THIS BOOK BELONGS TO
The Library of

....

....

I can't tell you how grateful I am that you decided to read my book. My most heartfelt thanks that you took time out of your life to choose my work and I hope you find benefit within these pages.

There are so many books available today that offer similar content so that makes it even more humbling that you decided to buying mine.

Tell me what you thought! I am eager to hear your opinion and ideas on what you read as are others who are looking for a good book to buy. Leave a review on Amazon.com so others can benefit from your wisdom!

With much thanks.

Table of Contents

SUMMARY

Crochet is a versatile and intricate art form that involves creating fabric by interlocking loops of yarn or thread using a crochet hook. It is a popular craft that has been practiced for centuries, with its origins dating back to the early 19th century.

The art of crochet allows for endless possibilities in terms of design and creativity. It can be used to create a wide range of items, including clothing, accessories, home decor, and even intricate lacework. The technique involves various stitches, each with its own unique look and texture, which can be combined to create intricate patterns and designs.

One of the key aspects of crochet is the use of a crochet hook, which is a specialized tool with a hooked end. The hook is used to pull loops of yarn through other loops, creating a chain of stitches. These stitches can then be built upon to create different patterns and textures. The size of the crochet hook and the thickness of the yarn or thread used can greatly influence the final outcome of the project, allowing for different levels of detail and drape.

Crochet patterns are typically made up of a combination of basic stitches, such as the chain stitch, single crochet, double crochet, and treble crochet. These stitches can be worked in different combinations and variations to create a wide range of textures and patterns. Additionally, more advanced techniques, such as colorwork, lacework, and Tunisian crochet, can be used to add even more complexity and visual interest to crochet projects.

One of the great advantages of crochet is its portability and accessibility. Unlike other crafts that may require large and bulky equipment, crochet can be done with just a hook and a small amount of yarn or thread. This makes it a popular choice for people who enjoy crafting on the go or in small spaces. Additionally, crochet is a relatively easy craft to learn, with many resources available online and in books to help beginners get started.

In recent years, crochet has experienced a resurgence in popularity, with many people embracing it as a way to express their creativity and create unique, handmade items. The rise of social media platforms, such as Instagram and Pinterest, has also contributed to the increased visibility of crochet, with many talented artists and designers sharing their work and inspiring others to try their hand at the craft.

Overall, the art of crochet is a beautiful and versatile craft that allows for endless possibilities in terms of design and creativity. Whether you're a beginner or an experienced crocheter, there is always something new to learn

Amigurumi is a Japanese art form that involves creating small, stuffed animals or objects using crochet or knitting techniques. The word amigurumi is derived from the Japanese words ami, meaning crocheted or knitted, and nuigurumi, meaning stuffed doll.

Amigurumi has gained immense popularity in recent years, not only in Japan but also around the world. This surge in popularity can be attributed to several factors. Firstly, amigurumi is a highly versatile craft that allows for endless creativity. With just a few basic crochet or knitting stitches, one can create a wide variety of adorable characters and objects. From cute animals like cats, dogs, and bears to whimsical creatures like unicorns and dragons, the possibilities are truly endless.

Furthermore, amigurumi appeals to people of all ages and skill levels. Whether you are a beginner or an experienced crocheter or knitter, you can easily learn and enjoy making amigurumi. The patterns for amigurumi are widely available, both in books and online, and often come with step-by-step instructions and helpful illustrations. This accessibility makes it a popular choice for those looking to try their hand at a new craft or hobby.

Another reason for the popularity of amigurumi is its inherent cuteness. The small size and soft texture of amigurumi creations make them incredibly adorable and appealing. They can be used as decorative items, toys for children, or even as keychains or accessories. The charm of amigurumi lies in its ability to bring joy and warmth to people's lives through these cute and lovable creations.

Additionally, amigurumi has gained a significant following on social media platforms such as Instagram and Pinterest. Many talented amigurumi artists and enthusiasts share their creations online, inspiring others and creating a sense of community. This online presence has further contributed to the popularity of amigurumi, as it allows for the exchange of ideas, patterns, and techniques among a global audience.

In conclusion, amigurumi has become a beloved craft worldwide due to its versatility, accessibility, cuteness, and online presence. Whether you are a beginner or an experienced crafter, amigurumi offers a creative outlet that brings joy and satisfaction. Its popularity is likely to continue growing as more people discover the joy of creating these adorable crochet or knitted creations.

To begin crocheting, you will need a variety of tools and materials. These items are essential for creating beautiful and intricate crochet projects. Here is a detailed list of the tools and materials you will need:

1. Crochet Hooks: These are the primary tools used in crochet. They come in various sizes, ranging from small to large, and are made from different materials such as aluminum, plastic, or wood. The size of the crochet hook you choose will depend on the thickness of the yarn you plan to use.

2. Yarn: Yarn is the main material used in crochet. It comes in a wide range of colors, textures, and thicknesses. When selecting yarn for your project, consider the pattern requirements and the desired outcome. Different yarns will produce different effects, so choose one that suits your project's needs.

3. Scissors: A good pair of sharp scissors is essential for cutting yarn and trimming loose ends. Make sure to have a dedicated pair of scissors for your crochet projects to keep them sharp and in good condition.

4. Stitch Markers: These small, removable markers are used to mark specific stitches or sections in your crochet work. They help you keep track of your progress and make it easier to follow complex patterns.

5. Tapestry Needles: These large-eyed needles are used for weaving in loose ends and sewing pieces together. They are essential for finishing your crochet projects neatly and securely.

6. Measuring Tape: A measuring tape is handy for checking the size and dimensions of your crochet work. It helps ensure that your project matches the required measurements specified in the pattern.

7. Stitch Holders: Stitch holders are used to hold stitches in place when you need to set aside a section of your work temporarily. They prevent stitches from unraveling and allow you to continue working on other parts of your project.

8. Row Counter: A row counter is a useful tool for keeping track of the number of rows you have completed. It eliminates the need to constantly count rows manually, especially in larger projects.

9. Blocking Tools: Blocking tools, such as blocking mats and pins, are used to shape and stretch your finished crochet projects. They help create a more professional and polished look by evening out stitches and ensuring that your project retains its intended shape.

Basic crochet stitches and techniques are the foundation of any crochet project. These stitches are the building blocks that allow you to create a wide variety of patterns and designs. Whether you are a beginner or an experienced crocheter, it is essential to have a solid understanding of these basic stitches in order to successfully complete any crochet project.

One of the most commonly used basic crochet stitches is the chain stitch. This stitch is the starting point for almost every crochet project. It is created by making a series of loops with the yarn and pulling the yarn through each loop to create a chain. The chain stitch is used to create the foundation row of a crochet project and is also used to create spaces and loops within a pattern.

Another important basic crochet stitch is the single crochet stitch. This stitch is created by inserting the hook into a stitch, yarn over, and pull through both loops on the hook. The single crochet stitch is used to create a dense and sturdy fabric and is often used in projects such as scarves, hats, and blankets.

The double crochet stitch is another commonly used basic crochet stitch. This stitch is created by yarn over, inserting the hook into a stitch, yarn over again, and pull through the first two loops on the hook. Yarn over again and pull through the remaining two loops on the hook. The double crochet stitch creates a taller stitch than the single crochet stitch and is often used to create lacy and openwork patterns.

In addition to these basic stitches, there are also various techniques that are important to learn in crochet. One such technique is changing colors. This technique allows you to create patterns and designs using different colored yarns. To change colors, you simply drop the current color and pick up the new color, leaving a tail of the old color to weave in later.

Another important technique is increasing and decreasing stitches. Increasing stitches allows you to add stitches to your project, while decreasing stitches allows you to remove stitches. These techniques are used to shape your crochet work and create curves and angles.

Blocking is another technique that is often used in crochet. Blocking involves wetting your finished crochet project and shaping it to the desired dimensions. This helps to even out stitches and give your project a more polished and professional look.

Overall, basic crochet stitches and techniques are essential for any crocheter. They provide the foundation for creating beautiful and intricate crochet projects. By mastering these stitches and techniques, you will be able to tackle more complex patterns and designs with confidence.

Amigurumi is a Japanese art form that involves creating small, stuffed crochet or knitted toys. The word amigurumi is derived from the Japanese words ami, meaning crocheted or knitted, and nuigurumi, meaning stuffed doll. These adorable creations are typically made using a single crochet stitch and are known for their cute and whimsical designs.

Amigurumi toys are often made using brightly colored yarns and are characterized by their large heads, small bodies, and exaggerated features. They can be made in various shapes and sizes, ranging from animals and creatures to inanimate objects and even fictional characters. The possibilities are endless when it comes to amigurumi, as crafters can let their imagination run wild and create unique and personalized toys.

The process of making amigurumi involves using a crochet hook or knitting needles to create individual stitches and rows, which are then joined together to form the desired shape. The toy is typically stuffed with fiberfill or other soft materials to give it a plush and huggable feel. Details such as facial features, limbs, and accessories are added using additional crochet or embroidery techniques.

Amigurumi has gained popularity worldwide due to its charm and versatility. It appeals to both children and adults alike, as these handmade toys can be used as decorative items, collectibles, or even as comforting companions. Many crafters enjoy the process of creating amigurumi as it allows them to express their creativity and bring their favorite characters or ideas to life.

In recent years, amigurumi has also become a popular trend in the crafting community, with numerous books, patterns, and online tutorials available to help beginners get started. The internet has played a significant role in the spread of amigurumi, as enthusiasts can easily share their creations, patterns, and tips with others around the world.

Overall, amigurumi is a delightful and enjoyable craft that combines the art of crochet or knitting with the joy of creating cute and lovable toys. Whether you are a seasoned crafter or a beginner looking to try something new, amigurumi offers endless possibilities for creativity and self-expression. So grab your crochet hook or knitting needles and start bringing your own amigurumi creations to life!

Creating amigurumi animals can be a fun and rewarding craft project. With step-by-step instructions, you can easily bring these adorable creatures to life. Here is a detailed guide on how to create a variety of amigurumi animals:

1. Gather your materials: To start, you will need some basic supplies. These include yarn in various colors, a crochet hook, stuffing, safety eyes or embroidery thread for the eyes, a yarn needle, and scissors. Make sure to choose soft and durable yarn suitable for amigurumi projects.

2. Choose your animal: Decide which animal you want to create. Popular choices include bears, rabbits, cats, dogs, and elephants. You can find patterns for specific animals online or in crochet books. Alternatively, you can create your own design by modifying existing patterns.

3. Read and understand the pattern: Carefully read through the pattern before you begin. Familiarize yourself with the stitches and techniques required. Make sure you understand any abbreviations or special instructions mentioned in the pattern.

4. Start with the body: Begin by creating the body of your amigurumi animal. This usually involves crocheting in the round to form a sphere or oval shape. Follow the pattern's instructions for the number of stitches and rounds needed. Use a stitch marker to keep track of your rounds.

5. Add limbs and features: Once the body is complete, it's time to add the limbs and features. This includes crocheting arms, legs, ears, and tails separately. Attach them to the body using the yarn needle. You can also add details like stripes, spots, or patches using different colored yarn.

6. Create the face: The face is an essential part of any amigurumi animal. Use safety eyes or embroider eyes using embroidery thread. Embroider a nose and mouth using a yarn needle and contrasting yarn. You can also add blush to the cheeks using a small amount of pink or red yarn.

7. Stuff and shape: Before closing up the amigurumi, stuff it firmly with polyester fiberfill or any other suitable stuffing material. Make sure to stuff evenly to achieve a symmetrical shape. Adjust the stuffing as needed to create the desired firmness.

8. Finish and assemble: Once the amigurumi is fully stuffed, close up any remaining openings using the yarn needle.

Crochet accessories are a popular and versatile way to add a touch of handmade charm to any outfit or home decor. Whether you're a seasoned crocheter or just starting out, there are endless possibilities for creating beautiful and unique accessories using this timeless craft.

Crochet accessories can range from simple and functional items like hats, scarves, and gloves, to more intricate and decorative pieces like shawls, bags, and jewelry. The beauty of crochet is that it allows you to experiment with different stitches, colors, and yarns to create one-of-a-kind accessories that reflect your personal style.

One of the great things about crochet accessories is that they can be made to fit any season or occasion. In the colder months, you can crochet cozy hats and scarves to keep warm, or stylish fingerless gloves for a trendy and practical accessory. In the warmer months, crochet shawls and lightweight bags can add a boho-chic touch to your summer wardrobe.

Not only are crochet accessories fashionable, but they also make for thoughtful and heartfelt gifts. Handmade accessories have a special quality that store-bought items simply can't replicate. By taking the time to crochet a gift for someone, you're showing them that you care and value their presence in your life.

Crochet accessories also offer a great opportunity to use up leftover yarn from other projects. Instead of letting those small scraps go to waste, you can incorporate them into a colorful and eclectic accessory. This not only reduces waste but also adds a unique and playful element to your crochet creations.

If you're new to crochet, don't worry! There are plenty of beginner-friendly patterns and tutorials available online to help you get started. With a little practice and patience, you'll soon be able to create your own stunning crochet accessories.

In conclusion, crochet accessories are a wonderful way to express your creativity and add a personal touch to your style. Whether you're making them for yourself or as gifts for loved ones, crochet accessories are sure to be cherished and appreciated. So grab your crochet hook and yarn, and let your imagination run wild as you embark on your crochet accessory journey.

Amigurumi animals are adorable crocheted or knitted stuffed toys that have gained immense popularity in recent years. They are not only loved by children but also by adults who appreciate their cuteness and charm. If you are a fan of amigurumi animals and want to incorporate them into accessories, there are several creative ways to do so.

One of the simplest ways to incorporate amigurumi animals into accessories is by attaching them to keychains or bag charms. You can crochet or knit a small amigurumi animal, such as a teddy bear or a bunny, and then attach it to a keychain ring or a lobster clasp. This way, you can carry your favorite amigurumi animal with you wherever you go, adding a touch of whimsy to your everyday items.

Another way to incorporate amigurumi animals into accessories is by sewing or crocheting them onto hats, scarves, or gloves. For example, you can sew a small amigurumi owl onto a beanie, creating a cute and unique winter accessory. Similarly, you can crochet a tiny amigurumi cat and attach it to the end of a scarf, making it a playful and eye-catching addition to your outfit.

If you are feeling more adventurous, you can even create amigurumi animal-inspired jewelry. For instance, you can crochet or knit small amigurumi animals and turn them into earrings or pendants. By attaching them to earring hooks or necklace chains, you can wear your favorite amigurumi animals as stylish and conversation-starting accessories.

Furthermore, you can incorporate amigurumi animals into home decor items. For example, you can crochet or knit a family of amigurumi animals and display them on a shelf or a mantelpiece. They can add a touch of whimsy and personality to your living space, making it feel cozy and inviting.

Incorporating amigurumi animals into accessories allows you to showcase your creativity and love for these adorable toys. Whether you choose to attach them to keychains, sew them onto clothing, create jewelry, or use them as home decor, the possibilities are endless. So, grab your crochet hook or knitting needles, choose your favorite amigurumi animal pattern, and start incorporating these charming creatures into your accessories today

A. Exploring more complex stitches and techniques can greatly enhance your skills as a crafter. By delving into these advanced techniques, you open up a world of possibilities for creating intricate and unique designs.

When you start exploring complex stitches, you will discover a whole new range of textures and patterns that can be incorporated into your projects. From cable stitches that create a twisted and braided effect, to lace stitches that add delicate and airy details, the options are endless. These stitches can elevate your work from simple and basic to sophisticated and eye-catching.

Not only do complex stitches add visual interest to your projects, but they also provide a challenge that can help you grow as a crafter. As you tackle more intricate patterns, you will develop a greater understanding of how stitches work together and how to manipulate them to achieve the desired effect. This increased knowledge and skill will allow you to take on more advanced projects in the future.

Exploring complex stitches also opens up opportunities for incorporating different techniques into your work. For example, you may come across stitches that require you to use multiple colors or yarn weights, or stitches that involve working in the round or creating three-dimensional shapes. By learning and practicing these techniques, you expand your repertoire and become a more versatile and well-rounded crafter.

Additionally, exploring complex stitches and techniques can be a source of inspiration and creativity. As you experiment with different stitches, you may discover new ways to combine them or modify them to create your own unique designs. This process of exploration and experimentation can spark your imagination and lead to innovative and original creations.

In conclusion, exploring more complex stitches and techniques is a valuable endeavor for any crafter. It not only enhances your skills and knowledge, but also opens up a world of possibilities for creating beautiful and unique projects. So, don't be afraid to dive into the world of complex stitches and techniques – you may be surprised at what you can achieve!

Crocheting gifts for birthdays, holidays, and celebrations is a wonderful way to show your creativity and thoughtfulness. Crochet, a versatile and enjoyable craft, allows you to create unique and personalized gifts that are sure to be cherished by your loved ones.

When it comes to birthdays, crocheted gifts can be tailored to suit the recipient's interests and preferences. For example, if your friend is a book lover, you can crochet a cozy book sleeve to protect their favorite novels. Alternatively, you can make a cute amigurumi toy in the shape of their favorite animal or character. The possibilities are endless, and the effort and time you put into creating a handmade gift will surely be appreciated.

Holidays are another perfect occasion to showcase your crochet skills. Whether it's Christmas, Easter, or Halloween, you can create festive decorations and accessories that add a touch of warmth and charm to any celebration. Crocheted ornaments, stockings, and wreaths can be hung on the Christmas tree or displayed around the house, creating a cozy and inviting atmosphere. For Easter, you can crochet adorable bunnies or colorful eggs to add a handmade touch to your decorations. And for Halloween, you can make spooky amigurumi creatures or crochet costumes for your little ones.

Celebrations such as weddings, anniversaries, and baby showers also provide opportunities to create meaningful crochet gifts. For weddings, you can crochet a beautiful lace shawl or a delicate ring bearer pillow. These handmade items can become cherished heirlooms that are passed down through generations. Anniversaries can be commemorated with crocheted blankets or afghans that symbolize the warmth and love shared by the couple. And for baby showers, you can crochet soft and cozy blankets, hats, and booties that will keep the little one warm and snug.

The beauty of crocheting gifts for birthdays, holidays, and celebrations is that you can customize them to suit the recipient's taste and style. You can choose their favorite colors, incorporate their hobbies or interests, and even add personal touches such as initials or names. This level of personalization makes crocheted gifts truly special and unique.

In addition to the joy of creating something with your own hands, crocheting gifts also allows you to give a gift that is sustainable and eco-friendly. By using yarn made from natural fibers or recycled materials, you can reduce your carbon footprint and contribute to a more sustainable future.

Photographing your crochet projects can be a fun and rewarding experience, allowing you to showcase your hard work and creativity. Whether you're looking to share your projects on social media, create a portfolio, or simply document your progress, there are several tips and techniques that can help you capture the beauty and intricacy of your crochet work.

1. Lighting: Good lighting is crucial for capturing clear and vibrant photos of your crochet projects. Natural light is often the best option, so try to photograph your projects near a window or outdoors during the day. Avoid using harsh overhead lighting or direct sunlight, as it can create unwanted shadows or wash out the colors.

If you're shooting indoors, you can use a softbox or a diffuser to create a more even and flattering light.

2. Background: Choose a background that complements your crochet project and enhances its visual appeal. A plain, neutral-colored background such as a white or light-colored wall, a wooden table, or a clean fabric can help your project stand out. Avoid busy or distracting backgrounds that may take away from the focus of your photo.

3. Composition: Pay attention to the composition of your photo to create visually pleasing images. Experiment with different angles, perspectives, and framing techniques to highlight the details and textures of your crochet work. Consider using the rule of thirds, where you divide your frame into a grid of nine equal parts and place the main subject along the intersecting lines or at their intersections.

4. Props and styling: Adding props or styling elements can enhance the overall aesthetic of your crochet project photos. Consider using items that complement the theme or colors of your project, such as yarn balls, crochet hooks, flowers, or other related accessories. However, be mindful not to overcrowd the photo or distract from the main subject.

5. Focus and depth of field: Ensure that your crochet project is in sharp focus by using the appropriate focus settings on your camera or smartphone. If you're using a DSLR or a camera with manual settings, consider using a wide aperture (low f-stop number) to create a shallow depth of field, which will blur the background and make your crochet work pop. On smartphones, you can achieve a similar effect by tapping on the subject to focus and then adjusting the exposure manually if needed.

The output of providing a recap of the key points from a book would involve summarizing and highlighting the most important aspects, themes, and events covered in the book. This would typically include a comprehensive overview of the plot, character development, and any significant messages or lessons conveyed by the author.

To begin, the recap would delve into the main storyline of the book, outlining the major events and plot twists that occur throughout. This would involve discussing the central conflict or problem that the protagonist faces, as well as the various obstacles and challenges they encounter along the way. The recap would also touch upon any subplots or secondary storylines that contribute to the overall narrative.

In addition to the plot, the recap would provide an analysis of the characters and their development throughout the book. This would involve discussing the main characters' motivations, personalities, and relationships with one another. It would also highlight any character arcs or transformations that occur, as well as the impact these changes have on the overall story.

Furthermore, the recap would explore the themes and messages conveyed by the author. This would involve identifying the underlying ideas or concepts that the book explores, such as love, friendship, power, or identity. The recap would then discuss how these themes are developed and explored throughout the book, and how they contribute to the overall meaning and impact of the story.

Additionally, the recap may touch upon the writing style and techniques used by the author. This could include discussing the use of imagery, symbolism, or foreshadowing, as well as any unique narrative structures or storytelling devices employed. By analyzing the author's writing choices, the recap would provide a deeper understanding of the book's literary merits and artistic qualities.

Overall, a detailed recap of the key points from a book would provide a comprehensive overview of the plot, character development, themes, and writing style. It would aim to capture the essence of the book and provide readers with a thorough understanding of its content and significance.

boy and girl

elephants

Unlike the stork, this pattern gives you the choice of a girl or a boy elephant. The differences between the two are their colors (brown for a boy and pink for a girl), and their accessories (flower for a girl and man-purse for a boy).

yarn

1 skein Cascade Yarns 220 Superwash (100% wool, 220 yds ea) in color #836 Pink (MC) for girl elephant 1 skein Cascade Yarns 220 Superwash (100% wool, 220 yds ea) in color #819 Brown (MC) for boy elephant 1 skein Cascade Yarns 220 Superwash (100% wool, 220 yds ea) in color #824 Yellow (CC1) for both 1 skein Dale of Norway Dale Baby Ull (100% wool, 192 yds ea) in color #0020 Off White (CC2) for accessories

hooks and notions

size F/5 (3.75mm) hook

size D/3 (3.25mm) hook

If necessary, change hook size to obtain gauge.

100% polyester fiberfill

1 pair 15 mm pink or brown animal eyes (Suzusei)

yellow glitter pom-pom (Darice)

white or pink pre-made foam heart(s) (Darice)

fabric glue

stitch marker

yarn needle

gauge

19 sc x 14 rows = 4" (10cm)

finished size

5½" (14cm) tall

notes

See Special Notes for information on working in the round and decreasing.

BODY

With MC and larger hook, ch 4, sl st in first ch to form ring.

RND 1: Ch 1, 6 sc into ring, place marker in last st to mark end of rnd. Do not join in first st—6 sc total.

RND 2: Work 2 sc in each st around, replace marker in last st throughout pattern —12 sc total.

RND 3: *Sc in next st, 2 sc in next st; rep from* around—18 sc total.

RND 4: *Sc in each of next 2 sts, 2 sc in next st; rep from* around—24 sc total.

RND 5: *Sc in each of next 3 sts, 2 sc in next st; rep from* around—30 sc total.

RND 6: *Sc in each of next 4 sts, 2 sc in next st; rep from* around—36 sc total.

RND 7: Sc in each st around.

RND 8: *Dec, sc in each of next 16 sts; rep from* once—34 sc total.

RNDS 9–14: Rep Rnd 7.

Sl st in next st. Fasten off and weave in ends.

BODY

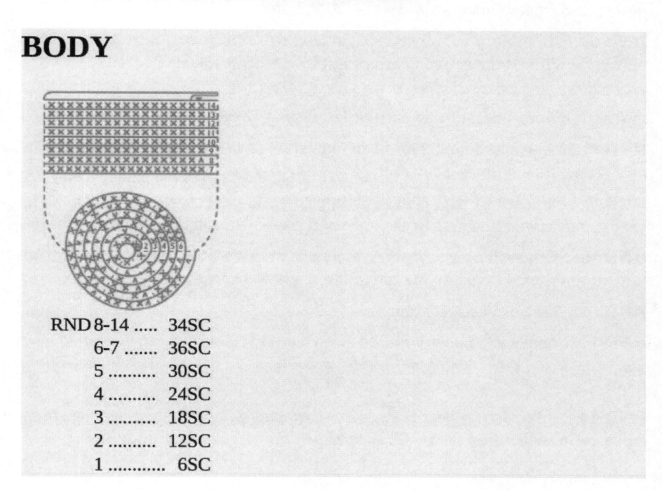

RND 8-14	34SC
6-7	36SC
5	30SC
4	24SC
3	18SC
2	12SC
1	6SC

HEAD

With MC and larger hook, ch 4, sl st in first ch to form ring.

RND 1: Ch 1, 6 sc into ring, place marker in last st to mark end of rnd. Do not join in first st—6 sc total.

RND 2: Work 2 sc in each st around, replace marker in last st throughout pattern —12 sc total.

RND 3: *Sc in next st, 2 sc in next st; rep from* around—18 sc total.

RND 4: Sc in next st, 2 sc in next st, *sc in each of next 2 sts, 2 sc in next st; rep from* 4 times, sc in last st—24 sc total.

RND 5: Sc in each of next 2 sts, 2 sc in next st, *sc in each of next 3 sts, 2 sc in next st; rep from* 4 times, sc in last st—30 sc total.

RND 6: Sc in each of next 2 sts, 2 sc in next st, *sc in each of next 4 sts, 2 sc in next st; rep from* 4 times, sc in each of last 2 sts—36 sc total.

RND 7: Sc in each of next 3 sts, 2 sc in next st, *sc in each of next 5 sts, 2 sc in next st; rep from* 4 times, sc in each of last 2 sts—42 sc total.

RND 8: Sc in each of next 3 sts, 2 sc in next st, *sc in each of next 6 sts, 2 sc in next st; rep from* 4 times, sc in each of last 3 sts—48 sc total.

RND 9: Sc in each of next 4 sts, 2 sc in next st, *sc in each of next 7 sts, 2 sc in next st; rep from* 4 times, sc in each of last 3 sts—54 sc total.

RND 10: Sc in each of next 4 sts, 2 sc in next st, *sc in each of next 8 sts, 2 sc in next st; rep from* 4 times, sc in each of last 4 sts—60 sc total.

RNDS 11–12: Sc in each st around.

RND 13: Change to smaller hook, sc in each of next 7 sts, dec, *sc in each of next 13 sts, sc 2 tog over next 2 sts; rep from* twice, sc in each of last 6 sts—56 sc total.

RND 14: Sc in each of next 6 sts, dec, *sc in each of next 12 sts, dec; rep from* twice, sc in each of last 6 sts—52 sc total.

RND 15: Rep Rnd 11.

RND 16: Sc in each of next 5 sts, dec, *sc in each of next 11 sts, dec; rep from* twice, sc in each of last 6 sts—48 sc total.

RND 17: Sc in each of next 4 sts, dec, *sc in each of next 10 sts, dec; rep from* twice, sc in each of last 6 sts—44 sc total.

RND 18: Rep Rnd 11.

RND 19: Sc in each of next 4 sts, dec, *sc in each of next 9 sts, dec; rep from* twice, sc in each of last 6 sts—40 sc total.

RND 20: Sc in each of next 3 sts dec, *sc in each of next 8 sts, dec; rep from* twice, sc in each of last 6 sts—36 sc total.

RND 21: Rep Rnd 11.

RND 22: Sc in each of next 2 sts, dec, *sc in each of next 8 sts, dec; rep from* twice, sc in each of last 2 sts—32 sc total.

RND 23: Sc in each of next 2 sts, dec, *sc in each of next 12 sts, dec; rep from* once—29 sc total.

RND 24: Rep Rnd 11.

Fasten off, leaving a long tail for sewing.

HEAD

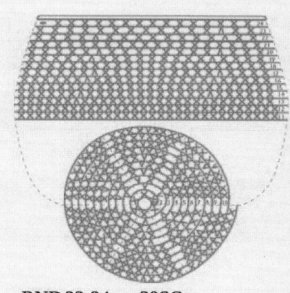

RND	23-24	30SC
	22	32SC
	20-21	36SC
	19	40SC
	17-18	44SC
	16	48SC
	14-15	52SC
	13	56SC
	10-12	60SC
	9	54SC
	8	48SC
	7	42SC

6	36SC
5	30SC
4	24SC
3	18SC
2	12SC
1	6SC

ARMS AND LEGS (make 4)

With CC1 and larger hook, ch 3, sl st in first ch to form ring.

RND 1: Ch 1, 6 sc into ring, place marker in last st to mark end of rnd. Do not join in first st—6 sc total.

RND 2: Work 2 sc in each st around, changing to MC with last st. Replace marker in last st throughout pattern— 12 sc total.

RND 3: Sc in each st around.

RND 4: Change to MC, *dec, sc in each of next 4 sts; rep from* once—10 sc total.

RNDS 5–7: Rep Rnd 3.

Sl st in next st. Fasten off, leaving a long tail for sewing.

ARMS & LEGS

RND 4-7	10SC
2-3	12SC
1	6SC

EARS

With MC and larger hook, ch 3, sl st in first ch to form ring.

RNDS 1–7: Work as for Rnds 1–7 of Body.

Sl st in next st. Fasten off, leaving a long tail for sewing.

EARS

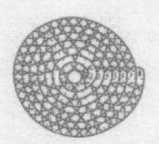

RND	6-7	....	36SC
	5	....	30SC
	4	....	24SC
	3	....	18SC
	2	....	12SC
	1	....	6SC

TRUNK

With MC and larger hook, ch 3, sl st in first ch to form ring.

RND 1: Ch 1, 6 sc into ring, place marker in last st to mark end of rnd. Do not join in first st—6 sc total.

RND 2: Work 2 sc in each st around. Replace marker in last st throughout pattern—12 sc total.

RNDS 3–4: Sc in each st around.

RND 5: *Dec, sc in each of next 4 sts; rep from* once—10 sc total.

RNDS 6–10: Rep Rnd 3.

Sl st in next st. Fasten off, leaving a long tail for sewing.

TRUNK

RND 5-10 ..... 10SC

    2-4 .... 12SC

    1 .... 6SC

MAN-PURSE (for Boy Elephant)

With larger hook and CC2, ch 4, sl st in first ch to form ring.

RND 1: Ch 1, 6 sc into ring, place marker in last st to mark end of rnd. Do not join in first st—6 sc total.

RND 2: Work 2 sc in each st around, replace marker in last st throughout pattern — 12 sc total.

RNDS 3–5: Sc in each st around.

Sl st in next st. Do not cut the yarn.

MAN-PURSE

RND 2-5 .... 12SC

    1 .... 6SC

STRAP

Ch 32. Fasten off, leaving a long tail. Sew to inside of mini purse on the opposite side.

FLOWER (for Girl Elephant)

With larger hook and CC2, ch 4, sl st in first ch to form ring. Work (ch 3, dc, ch 3, sl st) into ring 5 times—5 petals. Fasten off, leaving a long tail for sewing.

Assembly

Stuff all of the Body parts except the Ears, putting a small amount of stuffing into the Trunk. Then use tail ends and a yarn needle to sew the Ears (folded in half and Trunk to the Head. Attach the eyes to the Head. Use tail ends to sew the Head, Arms and Legs to the Body. Sew the Flower onto Girl Elephant's head. If desired, accent the center of the Flower with a bead or pom-pom. Weave in any loose ends.

sebastian

le hamster

Sebastian Le Hamster always wears his fancy beret. Place his eyes on round nine or ten, and place the nose in the vicinity of round twelve. Make sure the nose is precisely between the eyes. And give him an extra helping of stuffing before closing him up.

yarn

1 skein Bernat Cottontots (100% cotton, 171 yds ea) in color #128 Little Boy Blue (MC) 1 skein Bernat Cottontots (100% cotton, 171 yds ea) in color #7 Sweet Cream (CC1) 1 skein Bernat Cottontots (100% cotton, 171 yds ea) in color #615 Sunshine (CC2)

hooks and notions

size F/5 (3.75mm) hook

size D/3 (3.25mm) hook

If necessary, change hook size to obtain gauge.

stitch marker

yarn needle

100% polyester fiberfill

1 pair 15mm new blue plastic crystal eyes (Suzusei)

8mm plastic nose (Darice)

yellow glitter pom-pom (Darice)

gauge

16 sts x 12 rows = 4" (10cm) in sc using larger hook

finished size

7" (18cm) tall, including hat

notes

See Special Notes for information on working in the round and decreasing.

BODY

With larger hook and MC, ch 4, sl st in first ch to form ring.

RND 1: Ch 1, 6 sc into ring, place marker in last st to mark end of rnd. Do not join in first st—6 sc total.

RND 2: Work 2 sc in each st around, replace marker in last st throughout pattern —12 sc total.

RND 3: *Sc in next st, 2 sc in next st; rep from* around—18 sc total.

RND 4: *Sc in each of next 2 sts, 2 sc in next st; rep from* around—24 sc total.

RND 5: *Sc in each of next 3 sts, 2 sc in next st; rep from* around—30 sc total.

RND 6: *Sc in each of next 4 sts, 2 sc in next st; rep from* around—36 sc total.

RNDS 7–28: Sc in each st around.

RND 29: Changing to smaller crochet hook, *dec, sc in each of next 4 sts; rep from* around—30 sc total.

RND 30: *Dec, sc in each of next 3 sts; rep from* around— 24 sc total.

Begin stuffing the Body, continuing to add stuffing to desired fullness as you complete the Body.

RND 31: *Dec, sc in each of next 2 sts; rep from* around— 18 sc total.

RND 32: *Dec, sc in next st; rep from* around—12 sc total.

RND 33: Dec 6 times around—6 sc total.

Sl st in next st. Fasten off, leaving a long tail. Use a yarn needle to weave in ends.

BODY

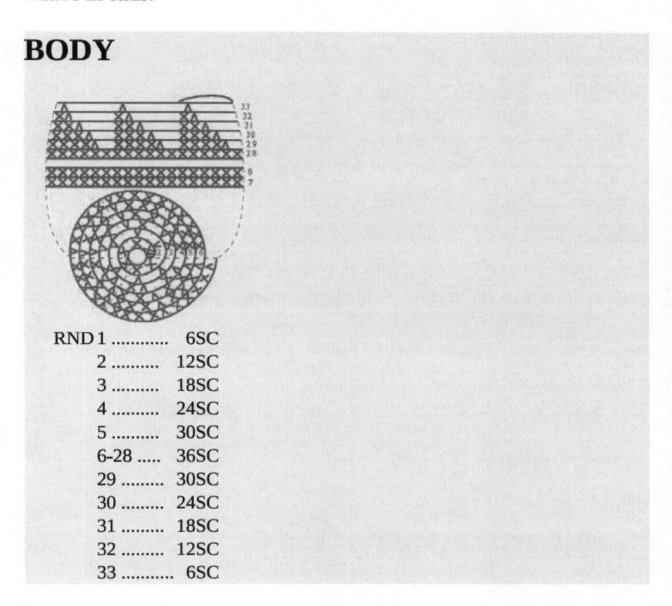

```
RND 1 ............    6SC
    2 ..........   12SC
    3 ..........   18SC
    4 ..........   24SC
    5 ..........   30SC
   6-28 .....    36SC
   29 ........   30SC
   30 .........   24SC
   31 .........   18SC
   32 .........   12SC
   33 ...........   6SC
```

ARMS AND LEGS (make 4)

With larger hook and CC1, ch 3, sl st in first ch to form ring.

RND 1: Ch 1, 5 sc into ring, place marker in last st to mark end of rnd. Do not join in first st—5 sc total.

RND 2: Sc in each st around, replace marker in last st throughout pattern.

RNDS 3–5: Sc in each st around.

Sl st in next st. Fasten off, leaving a long tail for sewing.

ARMS & LEGS

RND 1-5 .... 5SC

EARS (make 2)

With larger hook and CC1, ch 4, sl st in first ch to form ring.

RND 1: Work 8 sc into ring, place marker in last st to mark end of rnd. Do not join in first st—8 sc total.

RND 2: Sc in each st around, replace marker in last st throughout pattern.

RND 3: Sc in each st around.

Sl st in next st. Fasten off, leaving a long tail for sewing.

AROUND NOSE (make 1)

Work as for Ears.

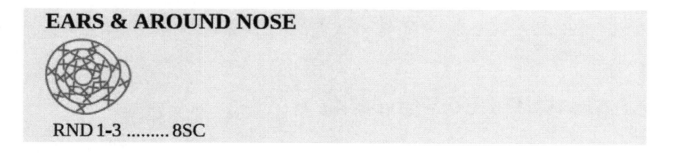

EARS & AROUND NOSE

RND 1-3 .... 8SC

BERET

With larger hook and CC2, ch 4, sl st in first ch to form ring.

RNDS 1–4: Work as for Rnds 1–4 of Body.

RND 5: Sc in each st around.

RND 6: *Dec, sc in each of next 3 sts; rep from* around, ending sc in each of last 2 sts—19 sc total.

Make sure the Body is firmly stuffed. Sl st in next st. Fasten off, leaving a long tail for sewing.

BERET

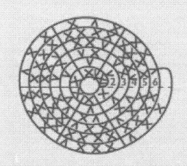

RND 1 .... 6SC
  2 .... 12SC
  3 .... 18SC
  4-5 .... 24SC
  6 .... 19SC

Assembly

Secure the plastic nose to Around Nose, and secure the plastic eyes to the Body. Use tail ends and a yarn needle to sew the Ears and Around Nose to the Body. Use tail ends to sew Arms, Legs and Beret to the Body. (Ears, Arms and Legs do not require stuffing.) Weave in any loose ends.

secure eyes at
Rnd 9 or 10

around Rnd 30,
begin stuffing Sebastian...
fill him up good

no stuffing needed for
Ears, Arms and Legs

spunky monkey and

pretty little kitty

A spunky, not-so-chunky monkey and a pretty little kitty can be made using the same pattern for the body, face, arms, legs and tail. Meow's wire whiskers make her stop going bananas and create absolute purrrfection.

yarn

1 skein Caron Perfect Match (100% acrylic, 355 yds ea) in Sunflower (MC for cat, CC for monkey) 1 skein Red Heart Super Saver (100% acrylic, 364 yds ea) in Aran (MC for monkey, CC for cat) *Plus scraps of yarn in colors of your choice for the scarves.*

hooks and notions

size F/5 (3.75mm) hook

size D/3 (3.25mm) hook
If necessary, change hook size to obtain gauge.

100% polyester fiberfill

24" (60cm) fun wire for cat's whiskers

1 pair 12mm yellow plastic cat's eyes for cat (Suzusei)

1 pair 12mm animal eyes for monkey (Suzusei)

8mm plastic nose each for monkey and cat (Darice)

pre-made red and white foam hearts (Darice)

stitch marker

yarn needle

fabric glue

gauge

16 sc x 11 rows = 4" (10cm) using larger hook

finished size

12" (30cm) tall, not including tail or ears

notes

See Special Notes for information on
working in the round and decreasing.

BODY (for Monkey and Cat)

With larger hook and CC, ch 4, sl st in first ch to form ring.

RND 1: Ch 1, 6 sc into ring, place marker in last st to mark end of rnd. Do not join in first st—6 sc total.

RND 2: Work 2 sc in each st around, replace marker in last st throughout pattern — 12 sc total.

RND 3: *Sc in next st, 2 sc in next st; rep from* around—18 sc total.

RND 4: *2 sc in next st, sc in each of next 2 sts; rep from* around—24 sc total.

RND 5: Sc in next st, 2 sc in next st, *sc in each of next 3 sts, 2 sc in next st; rep from* 4 times, sc in each of last 2 sts—30 sc total.

RNDS 6–7: Sc in each st around.

RND 8: *Sc in each of next 13 sts, dec; rep from* once—28 sc total.

RND 9: Sc in each of next 6 sts, dec, sc in each of next 12 sts, dec, sc in each st to end of rnd—26 sc total.

RND 10: Rep Rnd 6.

RND 11: Dec, sc in each of next 13 sts, dec, sc in each st to end of rnd—24 sc total.

RND 12: Rep Rnd 6.

RND 13: Sc in each of next 4 sts, dec, sc in each of next 10 sts, dec, sc in each st to end of rnd—22 sc total.

RND 14: Rep Rnd 6.

RND 15: Dec, sc in each of next 9 sts, dec, sc in each st to end of rnd—20 sc total.

RND 16: Rep Rnd 6.

RND 17: Sc in each of next 2 sts, dec, sc in each of next 8 sts, dec, sc in each st to end of rnd—18 sc total.

RND 18: Rep Rnd 6.

Sl st in next st. Fasten off and weave in ends.

BODY (MONKEY & CAT)

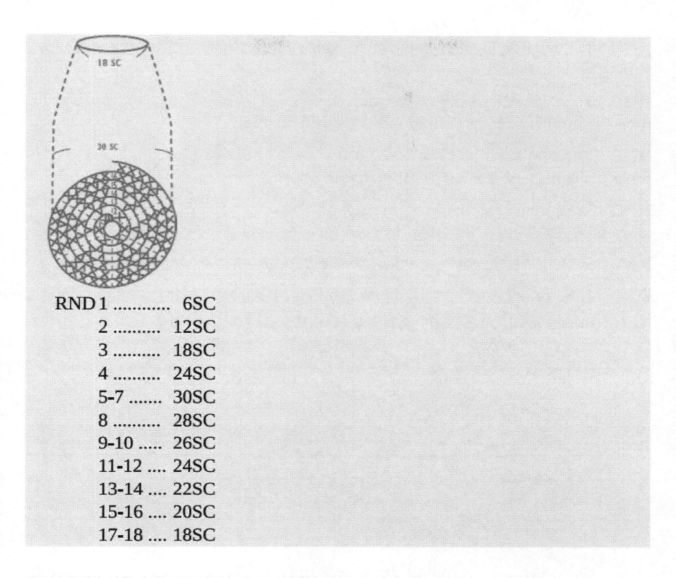

RND 1 .... 6SC
2 .... 12SC
3 .... 18SC
4 .... 24SC
5-7 .... 30SC
8 .... 28SC
9-10 ..... 26SC
11-12 .... 24SC
13-14 .... 22SC
15-16 .... 20SC
17-18 .... 18SC

HEAD (for Monkey and Cat)

With larger hook and MC, ch 4, sl st in first ch to form ring.

RNDS 1–5: Work as for Rnds 1–5 of Body.

RND 6: Sc in each of next 3 sts, 2 sc in next, *sc in each of next 4 sts, 2 sc in next st; rep from* 4 times, sc in last st of rnd—36 sc total.

RND 7: *Sc in each of next 5 sts, 2 sc in next; rep from* 5 times—42 sc total.

RND 8: *2 sc in next st, sc in each of next 6 sts; rep from* 5 times—48 sc total.

RNDS 9–10: Sc in each st around.

RND 11: *Sc in each of next 22 sts, dec; rep from* once—46 sc total.

RND 12: Switch to smaller hook, *sc in each of next 7 sts, dec; rep from* 4 times, ending with sc in last st—41 sc total.

RND 13: Sc in each of next 5 sts, dec, *sc in each of next 6 sts, dec; rep from* 3 times, ending with sc in each of last 2 sts—36 sc total.

RND 14: Sc in each of next 3 sts, dec, * sc in each of next 5 sts, dec; rep 3 times, sc in each of last 3 sts—31 sc total.

RND 15: Sc in next st, dec, * sc in each of next 4 sts, dec; rep from * 3 times, sc in each of last 4 sts—26 sc total.

RND 16: Dec, * sc in each of next 4 sts, dec; rep from * around—21 sc total.

RND 17: Sc in next st, * dec, sc in each of next 2 sts; rep from * around.

Sl st in next st. Fasten off, leaving a long tail for sewing.

HEAD (MONKEY & CAT)

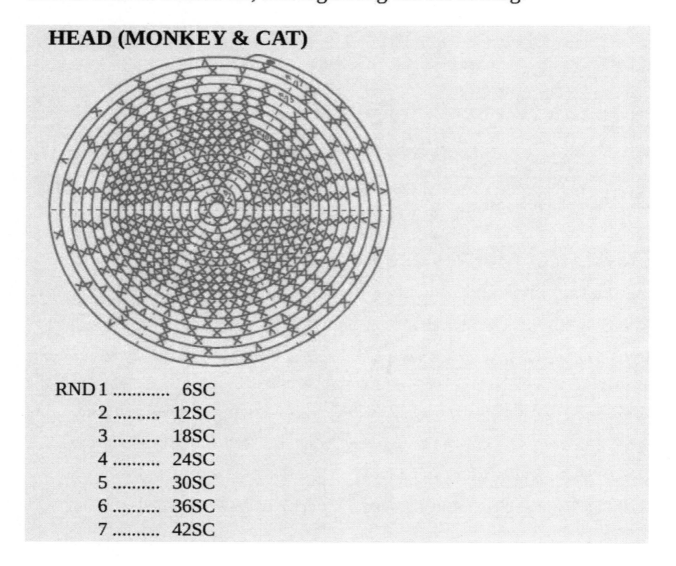

RND 1	6SC
2	12SC
3	18SC
4	24SC
5	30SC
6	36SC
7	42SC

8-10	48SC
11	46SC
12	41SC
13	36SC
14	31SC
15	26SC
16	21SC
17	16SC

◖ slip stitch ◖ chain ✕ single chrochet ∨ 2 single chrochet in one ∧ 1 single chrochet

LEGS AND ARMS (make 4 each for Monkey and Cat)

With larger hook and CC, ch 4, sl st in first ch to form ring.

RND 1: Ch 1, 6 sc into ring, place marker in last st to mark end of rnd. Do not join in first st—6 sc total.

RND 2: Work 2 sc in each st around, replace marker in last st throughout pattern —12 sc total.

RND 3: Sc in each st around.

RND 4: Switch to smaller hook and MC, * sc in each of next 2 sts, dec; rep from * around—9 sc total.

RNDS 5–21: Switch to larger hook, sc in each st around.

RND 22: Sc in each st around to last st, sl st in last st.

Sl st in next st. Fasten off, leaving a long tail for sewing.

LEGS & ARMS (CAT & MONKEY)

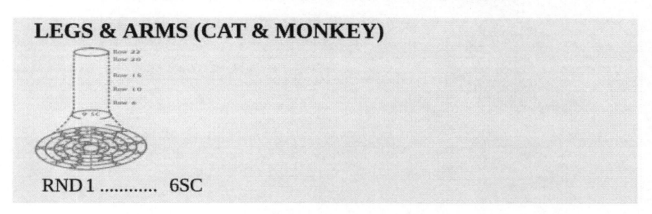

RND 1 .... 6SC

| 2 | ..... | 12SC |
| 4-22 | ...... | 9SC |

TAIL (for Monkey and Cat)

With larger hook and MC, ch 4, sl st in first ch to form ring.

RND 1: Work 7 sc into ring, place marker in last st to mark end of rnd. Do not join in first st—7 sc total.

RNDS 2–25: Sc in each st around, replace marker in last st throughout pattern. Sl st in next st. Fasten off, leaving a long tail for sewing.

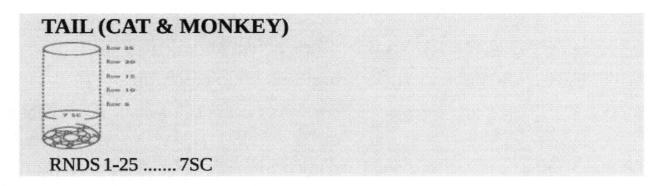

TAIL (CAT & MONKEY)

RNDS 1-25 .... 7SC

FACE (for Monkey)

With CC, work Rnds 1–6 as for Head.
Sl st in next st. Fasten off, leaving a long tail for sewing.

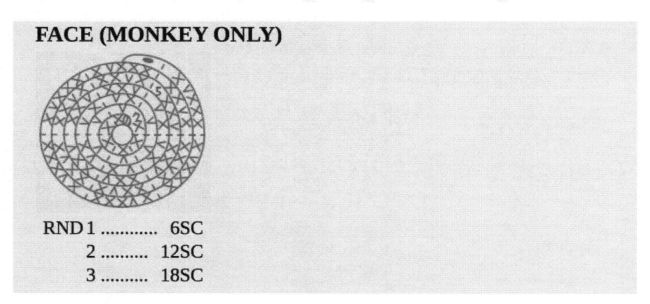

FACE (MONKEY ONLY)

RND 1	....	6SC
2	....	12SC
3	....	18SC

4	....	24SC
5	....	30SC
6	....	36SC

MONKEY EARS (make 2)

With larger hook and MC, ch 4, sl st in first ch to form ring.

RND 1: Ch 1, 6 sc into ring, place marker in last st to mark end of rnd. Do not join in first st—6 sc total.

RND 2: Work 2 sc in each st around, replace marker in last st throughout pattern —12 sc total.

RNDS 3–4: Sc in each st around.

Sl st in next st. Fasten off, leaving a long tail for sewing.

EARS (MONKEY ONLY)

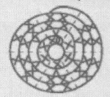

| RND 1 | .... | 6SC |
| 2-4 | .... | 12SC |

CAT EARS (make 2)

With larger hook and CC, ch 4, sl st in first ch to form ring.

RND 1: Ch 1, 6 sc into ring, place marker in last st to mark end of rnd. Do not join in first st—6 sc total.

RND 2: Sc in each st around, replace marker in last st throughout pattern—6 sc total.

RND 3: Work 2 sc in each st around—12 sc total.

RND 4: Rep Rnd 2.

RND 5: *Sc in next st, 2 sc in next st; rep from* around—18 sc total.

RNDS 6–7: Rep Rnd 2.

Sl st in next st. Fasten off, leaving a long tail for sewing.

EARS (CAT ONLY)

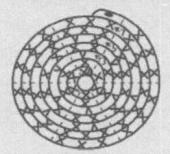

RND 1-2 .... 26SC
3-4 .... 12SC
5-7 .... 18SC

ASSEMBLY

Spunky Monkey

Stuff all of the parts except for the Ears with fiberfill. Secure the plastic eyes and nose to the Face. Use tail ends and a yarn needle to sew the Face and Ears to the Head. Use tail ends to sew the Head, Arms, Legs and Tail to the Body. Weave in any loose ends. Use fabric glue to adhere foam hearts to Monkey's chest, if desired.

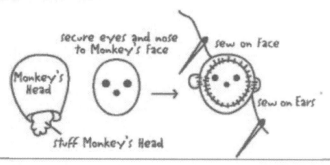

ASSEMBLY

Pretty Little Kitty

Stuff all of the parts except the Ears with fiberfill, as for the Monkey. Secure the plastic eyes to the Head. Follow the construction diagram to secure the whiskers to the Cat's Face. Use tail ends and a yarn needle to sew the Ears to the Head. Use tail ends to sew the Head, Arms, Legs and Tail to the Body. Weave in any loose ends. Use fabric glue to adhere foam hearts to Kitty's chest, if desired.

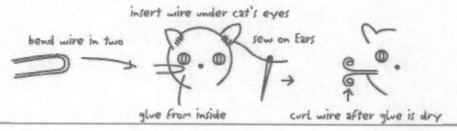

panda bear

keychains

One of these keychains makes the perfect accessory for your Porsche or Vespa, mansion or houseboat. This is a small yet delicate project that requires patience and attention to detail. Attach the key holder onto the head of the panda bear and keep it snug with the scarf.

yarn

1 skein Bernat Baby (100% acrylic, 286 yds ea) in color #402 White (MC) 1 skein Bernat Baby (100% acrylic, 286 yds ea) in color #451 Baby Blue (boy) or color #469 Pink (girl) (CC1) scraps of Cascade 220 superwash (100% wool) in color #836 Pink (for girl's scarf) and in color #824 Yellow (for boy's scarf)

hooks and notions

size C/2 (2.75mm) hook

size B/1 (2.25mm) hook

If necessary, change hook size to obtain gauge.

stitch marker

yarn needle

1 pair 4mm google eyes in pink or blue (Suzusei)

4mm nose (Darice)

100% polyester fiberfill

key ring

fabric glue

gauge

20 sc x 22 rows = 4" (10cm) with larger hook

24 sc x 25 rows = 4" (10cm) with smaller hook

finished size

3½" (9cm) tall

notes

See Special Notes for information on working in the round and decreasing.

HEAD

With MC and larger hook, ch 3, sl st in first ch to form ring.

RND 1: Ch 1, 6 sc into ring, place marker in last st to mark end of rnd. Do not join in first st—6 sc total.

RND 2: Work 2 sc in each st around, replace marker in last st throughout pattern —12 sc total.

RND 3: *Sc in next st, 2 sc in next st; rep from* around— 18 sc total.

RND 4: *2 sc in next st, sc in each of next 2 sts; rep from* around—24 sc total.

RND 5: Sc in next st, *2 sc in next st, sc in each of next 3 sts; rep from* around, ending sc in each of last 2 sts—30 sc total.

RND 6: Sc in each of next 3 sts, *2 sc in next st, sc in each of next 4 sts; rep from* around, ending with sc in last st—36 sc total.

RND 7: Sc in each st around.

RND 8: *Sc in each of next 16 sts, dec; rep from* once— 34 sc total.

RND 9: Switch to smaller hook, *sc in each of next 5 sts, dec; rep from* 3 times, sc in each of last 6 sts—30 sc total.

RND 10: *Dec, sc in each of next 4 sts; rep from* around—25 sc total.

RND 11: *Dec, sc in each of next 3 sts; rep from* around—20 sc total.

RND 12: *Dec, sc in each of next 2 st; rep from* around— 15 sc total.

Sl st in next st. Fasten off, leaving a long tail for sewing.

HEAD

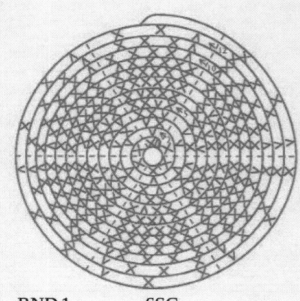

RND 1 .... 6SC
    2 .... 12SC
    3 .... 18SC
    4 .... 24SC

5	30SC
6-7	36SC
8	34SC
9	30SC
10	25SC
11	20SC
12	15SC

BODY

With MC and smaller hook, ch 3, sl st in first ch to form ring.

RNDS 1–5: Work as for Rnds 1–5 of Head.

RND 6: Sc in each st around.

RND 7: *Sc in each of next 14 sts, 2 sc in next st; rep from* once—32 sc total.

RNDS 8–9: Rep Rnd 6.

RND 10: Dec, sc in each of next 10 sts, dec, sc in each st around—30 sc total.

RND 11: Sc in each of next 6 sts, dec, sc in each of next 11 sts, dec, sc in each st around—28 sc total.

RND 12: Rep Rnd 6.

RND 13: Dec, sc in each of next 8 sts, dec, sc in each st around—26 sc total.

RND 14: Sc in each of next 5 sts, dec, sc in each of next 9 sts, dec, sc in each st around—24 sc total.

RND 15: Dec, sc in each of next 6 sts, dec, sc in each st around—22 sc total.

RND 16: Sc in each of next 4 sts, dec, sc in each of next 7 sts, dec, sc in each st around—20 sc total.

Sl st in next st. Fasten off and weave in ends.

BODY

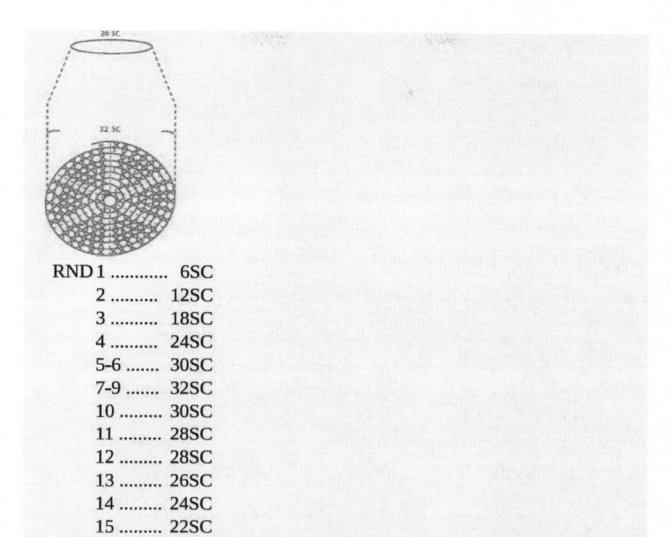

RND 1 .... 6SC
2 .... 12SC
3 .... 18SC
4 .... 24SC
5-6 .... 30SC
7-9 .... 32SC
10 .... 30SC
11 .... 28SC
12 .... 28SC
13 .... 26SC
14 .... 24SC
15 .... 22SC
16 .... 20SC

ARMS AND LEGS (make 4)

With CC and smaller hook, ch 3, sl st in first ch to form ring.

RND 1: Ch 1, 6 sc into ring, place marker in last st to mark end of rnd. Do not join in first st—6 sc total.

RNDS 2–7: Sc in each st around, replace marker in last st throughout pattern. Sl st in next st. Fasten off, leaving a long tail for sewing.

ARMS & LEGS

RND 1-7 .... 6SC

EARS (make 2)

With CC and smaller hook, ch 3, sl st in first ch to form ring.

RND 1: Ch 1, 5 sc into ring, place marker in last st to mark end of rnd. Do not join in first st—5 sc total.

RND 2: Work 2 sc in each st around, replace marker in last st throughout pattern —10 sc total.

RNDS 3–4: Sc in each st around.

Sl st in next st. Fasten off, leaving a long tail for sewing.

EARS

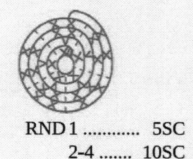

RND 1 .... 5SC
   2-4 .... 10SC

AROUND EYES (make 2)

With CC and smaller hook, ch 3, sl st in first ch to form ring.

RND 1: Work 6 sc into ring, sl st in first sc to join—6 sc total.

Fasten off, leaving a long tail for sewing.

AROUND EYES

RND 1 .... 6SC

Assembly

Stuff all parts except the Ears with fiberfill, and use tail ends and a yarn needle to sew the Ears and Around Eyes (after eyes are glued on) to the Head. Secure the plastic nose between the eyes. Using tail ends, sew the Head, Arms and Legs to the Body. Weave in any loose ends.

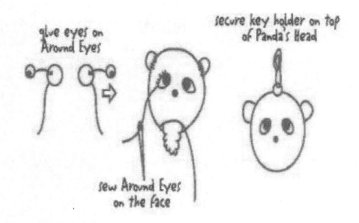

glue eyes on
Around Eyes

sew Around Eyes
on the face

secure key holder on top
of Panda's Head

the real

yarn

1 skein Red Heart Super Saver (100% acrylic, 364 yds ea) in Fuchsia (MC) 1 skein Red Heart Super Saver (100% acrylic, 364 yds ea) in Aran (CC) light pink scrap yarn for scarf

hooks and notions

size F/5 (3.75mm) hook

size D/3 (3.25mm) hook

If necessary, change hook size to obtain gauge.

100% polyester fiberfill

stitch marker

yarn needle

1 pair 30mm comical eyes (Suzusei)

8mm black nose (Darice)

pre-made red and pink foam hearts (Darice)

fabric glue

gauge

16 sc x 11 rows = 4" (10cm) with larger hook

finished size

10" (25cm) tall

notes

See Special Notes for information on working in the round and decreasing.

HEAD

With larger hook and MC, ch 4, sl st in first ch to form ring.

RND 1: Ch 1, 7 sc into ring, place marker in last st to mark end of rnd. Do not join in first st—7 sc total.

RND 2: Work 2 sc in each st around, replace marker in last st throughout pattern —14 sc total.

RND 3: *Sc in next st, 2 sc in next st; rep from* around—21 sc total.

RND 4: *2 sc in next st, sc in each of next 2 sts; rep from* around—28 sc total.

RND 5: Sc in each of next 2 sts, 2 sc in next st, *sc in each of next 3 sts, 2 sc in next st; rep from* around, ending with sc in last st—35 sc total.

RND 6: *Sc in each of next 4 sts, 2 sc in next st; rep from* around—42 sc total.

RND 7: *2 sc in next st, sc in each of next 5 sts; rep from* around—49 sc total.

RND 8: Sc in each of next 2 sts, 2 sc in next st, *sc in each of next 6 sts, 2 sc in next st; rep from* around, ending sc in each of last 4 sts—56 sc total.

RND 9: Sc in each of next 4 sts, 2 sc in next, *sc in each of next 7 sts, 2 sc in next* *st; rep from* around, ending with sc in each of last 3 sts—63 sc total.

RND 10: Sc in each of next 6 sts, 2 sc in next, *sc in each of next 8 sts, 2 sc in next st; rep from* around, ending sc in each of last 2 sts—70 sc total.

RNDS 11–15: Sc in each st around.

RND 16: Switch to smaller hook, *sc in each of next 8 sts, dec; rep from* around —63 sc total.

RND 17: Sc in each of next 3 sts, dec, *sc in each of next 7 sts, dec; rep from* around, ending sc in last 4 sts—56 sc total.

RND 18: *Sc in each of next 6 sts, dec; rep from* around—49 sc total.

RND 19: Sc in each of next 2 sts, dec, *sc in each of next 5 sts, dec; rep from* around, ending sc in each of last 3 sts—42 sc total.

RND 20: *Sc in each of next 4 sts, dec; rep from* around— 35 sc total.

RND 21: Sc in next st, dec, *sc in each of next 3 sts, dec; rep from* around, sc in each of last 2 sts—28 sc total.

RND 22: *Sc in each of next 5 sts, dec; rep from* around— 24 sc total.

RND 23: Sc in each st around.

Sl st in next st. Fasten off, leaving a long tail for sewing.

HEAD

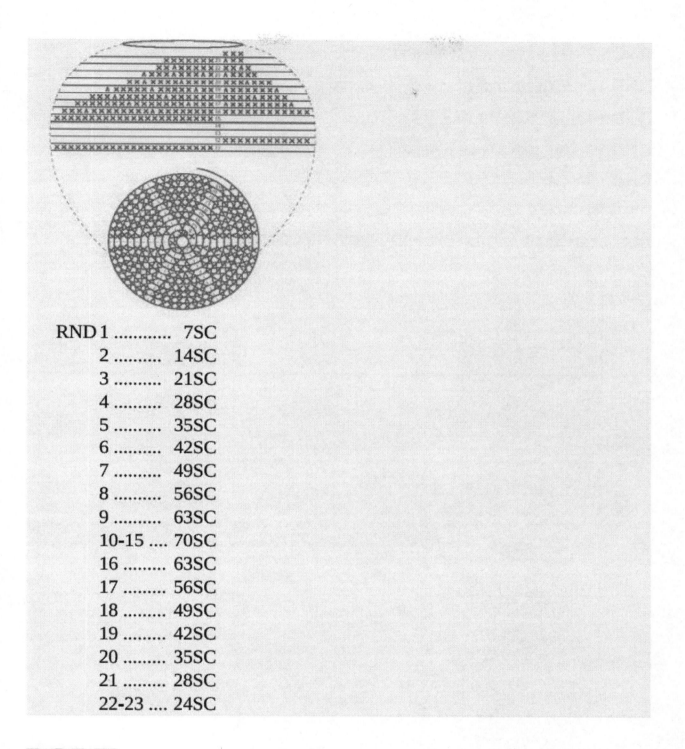

RND 1 .... 7SC
2 .... 14SC
3 .... 21SC
4 .... 28SC
5 .... 35SC
6 .... 42SC
7 .... 49SC
8 .... 56SC
9 .... 63SC
10-15 .... 70SC
16 .... 63SC
17 .... 56SC
18 .... 49SC
19 .... 42SC
20 .... 35SC
21 .... 28SC
22-23 .... 24SC

BODY

With larger hook and CC, ch 4, sl st in first ch to form ring.

RNDS 1–6: Work as for Rnds 1–6 of Head.

RNDS 7–11: Sc in each st around.

RND 12: *Sc in each of next 4 sts, dec; rep from* around—35 sc total.

RNDS 13–18: Rep Rnd 7.

RND 19: *Dec, sc in each of next 3 sts; rep from* around— 28 sc total.

RNDS 20–24: Rep Rnd 7.

RND 25: *Sc in each of next 5 sts, dec; rep from* around— 24 sc total. Sl st in next st. Fasten off and weave in ends.

BODY

RND 1 .... 7SC
2 .... 14SC
3 .... 21SC
4 .... 28SC
5 .... 35SC
6-11 ..... 42SC
12-18 .... 35SC
19-24 .... 28SC
25 .... 24SC

EARS (make 2)

With larger hook and CC, ch 4, sl st in first ch to form ring.

RND 1: Ch 1, 6 sc into ring, place marker in last st to mark end of rnd. Do not join in first st—6 sc total.

RND 2: Work 2 sc in each st around, replace marker in last st throughout pattern —12 sc total.

RND 3: *Sc in next st, 2 sc in next st; rep from* around— 18 sc total.

RNDS 4–5: Sc in each st around.

Sl st in next st. Fasten off, leaving a long tail for sewing.

EARS

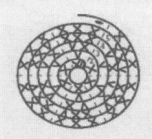

RND 1 .... 6SC
    2 .... 12SC
  3-5 .... 18SC

AROUND NOSE

With larger hook and CC, ch 4, sl st in first ch to form ring.

RND 1: Ch 1, 7 sc into ring, place marker in last st to mark end of rnd. Do not join in first st—7 sc total.

RND 2: Work 2 sc in each st around, replace marker in last st throughout pattern —14 sc total.

RND 3: *Sc in next st, 2 sc in next st; rep from* around— 21 sc total.

Sl st in next st. Fasten off, leaving a long tail for sewing. Attach plastic nose to the Around Nose section.

AROUND NOSE

RND 1 .... 7SC

2 .... 14SC

3 .... 21SC

LEGS (make 2)

With larger hook and CC, ch 4, sl st in first ch to form ring.

RND 1: Ch 1, 8 sc into ring, place marker in last st to mark end of rnd. Do not join in first st—8 sc total.

RND 2: Work 2 sc in each st around, replace marker in last st throughout pattern —16 sc total.

RND 3: Sc in each st around.

RNDS 4–6: Switch to MC, sc in each st around.

RND 7: Dec, sc in each st around—15 sc total.

RNDS 8–10: Sc in each st around.

RND 11: Rep Rnd 7—14 sc total.

RND 12: Rep Rnd 8.

Sl st in next st. Fasten off, leaving a long tail for sewing.

LEGS

RND 1	....	8SC
2-6	....	16SC
7-10	.....	15SC
11-12	....	14SC

ARMS (make 2)

With larger hook and CC, ch 4, sl st in first ch to form ring.

RND 1: Ch 1, 5 sc into ring, place marker in last st to mark end of rnd. Do not join in first st—5 sc total.

RND 2: Work 2 sc in each st around, replace marker in last st throughout pattern —10 sc total.

RND 3: Sc in each st around.

RNDS 4–12: Switch to MC, sc in each st around.

RND 13: Dec, sc in each st around—9 sc total.

RNDS 14–15: Rep Rnd 4.

Sl st in next st. Fasten off, leaving a long tail for sewing.

ARMS

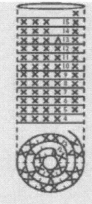

RND 1 .... 5SC

2-12 ..... 10SC

13-15 ...... 9SC

Assembly

Stuff the Head with fiberfill. Then secure the plastic eyes to the Head. Use tail ends and a yarn needle to sew the Ears and Around Nose to the Head. Use tail ends to sew the Head, Arms and Legs to the Body. Weave in any loose ends.

curve the Ears a little when sewing to Head

sew on Around Nose... no stuffing needed

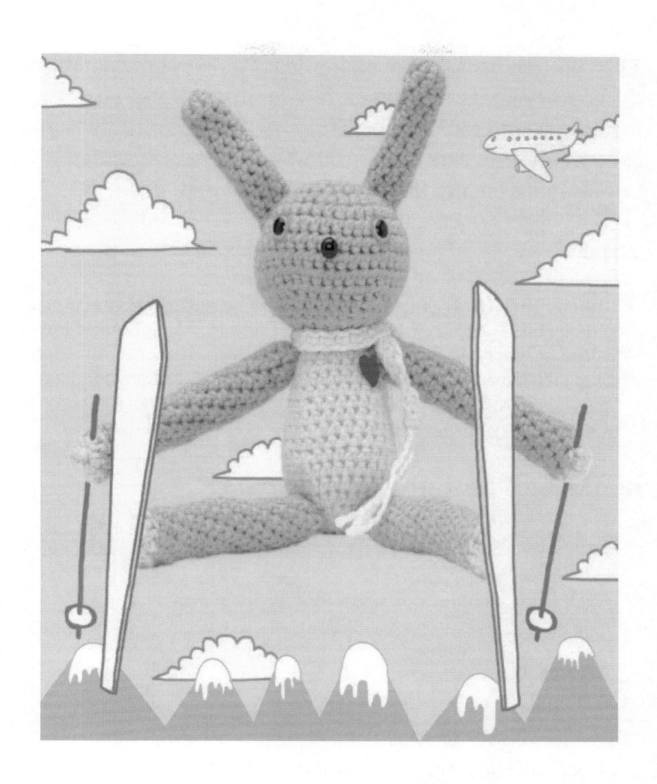

a hare
     and a **bear**

This pattern is a good example of how you can make different animals with just a few modifications. The body, face, arms and legs of the Hare and the Bear are the same except for the ears and around the nose. Symmetry is important to ensure this Hare and Bear look just right.

yarn

1 skein Red Heart Super Saver (100% acrylic, 364 yds ea) in Spruce (MC for Hare, CC for Bear) 1 skein Red Heart Super Saver (100% acrylic, 364 yds ea) in Aran (CC for Hare, MC for Bear) scrap of Bernat Cottontots (100% cotton) in Sunshine for Hare's Scarf scrap of Lion Brand Landscapes (wool/acrylic blend) in Summer Fields for Bear's Scarf

hooks and notions

size F/5 (3.75mm) hook

size D/3 (3.25mm) hook
If necessary, change hook size to obtain gauge.

stitch marker

yarn needle

100% polyester fiberfill

8mm plastic nose (Darice)

1 pair 12mm moss green animal eyes for Bear

(Suzusei)

1 pair 12mm animal eyes for Hare

pre-made red foam heart(s) (Darice)

fabric glue

gauge

16 sc x 11 rows = 4" (10cm) with larger hook

finished size

10¾" (27cm) tall (not including ears)

notes

See Special Notes for information on working in the round and decreasing.

BODY (for Hare and Bear)

With larger hook and CC, ch 4, sl st in first ch to form ring.

RND 1: Ch 1, 6 sc into ring, place marker in last st to mark end of rnd. Do not join in first st—6 sc total.

RND 2: Work 2 sc in each st around, replace marker in last st throughout pattern —12 sc total.

RND 3: *Sc in next st, 2 sc in next st; rep from* around—18 sc total.

RND 4: *2 sc in next st, sc in each of next 2 sts; rep from* around—24 sc total.

RND 5: Sc in next st, 2 sc in next st, *sc in each of next 3 sts, 2 sc in next st; rep from* 4 times, sc in each of last 2 sts—30 sc total.

RNDS 6–7: Sc in each st around.

RND 8: *Sc in each of next 13 sts, dec; rep from* once—28 sc total.

RND 9: Sc in each of next 6 sts, dec, sc in each of next 12 sts, dec, sc in each st to end of rnd—26 sc total.

RNDS 10–11: Rep Rnd 6.

RND 12: Dec, sc in each of next 13 sts, dec, sc in each st to end of rnd—24 sc total.

RND 13: Sc in each of next 4 sts, dec, sc in each of next 10 sts, dec, sc in each st to end of rnd—22 sc total.

RND 14: Rep Rnd 6.

RND 15: Dec, sc in each of next 9 sts, dec, sc in each st to end of rnd—20 sc total.

RND 16: Sc in each of next 2 sts, dec, sc in each of next 8 sts, dec, sc in each st to end of rnd—18 sc total.

RND 17: Rep Rnd 6.

Sl st in next st. Fasten off and weave in ends.

BODY (HARE & BEAR)

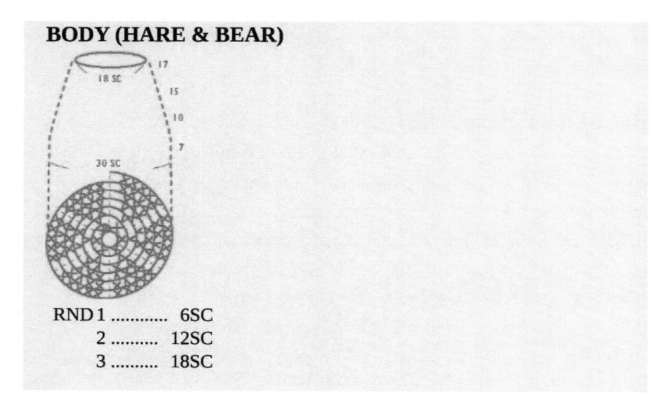

RND 1 .... 6SC

2 .... 12SC

3 .... 18SC

```
4 .......... 24SC
5-7 ....... 30SC
8 .......... 28SC
9-11 ..... 26SC
12 ......... 24SC
13-14 .... 22SC
15 ......... 20SC
16-17 .... 18SC
```

✕ Single Chrochet ∧ Decreasing 2 SC in 1 SC

∨ Increasing 1 SC to 2 SC

● slip stitch

HEAD (for Hare and Bear)

With larger hook and MC, ch 4, sl st in first ch to form ring.

RNDS 1–5: Work as for Rnds 1–5 of Body.

RND 6: Sc in each of next 3 sts, 2 sc in next, *sc in each of next 4 sts, 2 sc in next st; rep from* 4 times, sc in last st of rnd—36 sc total.

RND 7: *Sc in each of next 5 sts, 2 sc in next; rep from* 5 times—42 sc total.

RNDS 8–9: Sc in each st around.

RND 10: *Sc in each of next 19 sts, dec; rep from* once— 40 sc total.

RND 11: Switch to smaller hook, *sc in each of next 6 sts, dec; rep from* around —35 sc total.

RND 12: *Sc in each of next 5 sts, dec; rep from* around—30 sc total.

RND 13: *Sc in each of next 4 sts, dec; rep from* around—25 sc total.

RND 14: *Sc in each of next 3 sts, dec; rep from* around—20 sc total.

RND 15: *Sc in each of next 2 sts, dec; rep from* around—14 sc total.

Sl st in next st. Fasten off, leaving a long tail for sewing.

HEAD (HARE & BEAR)

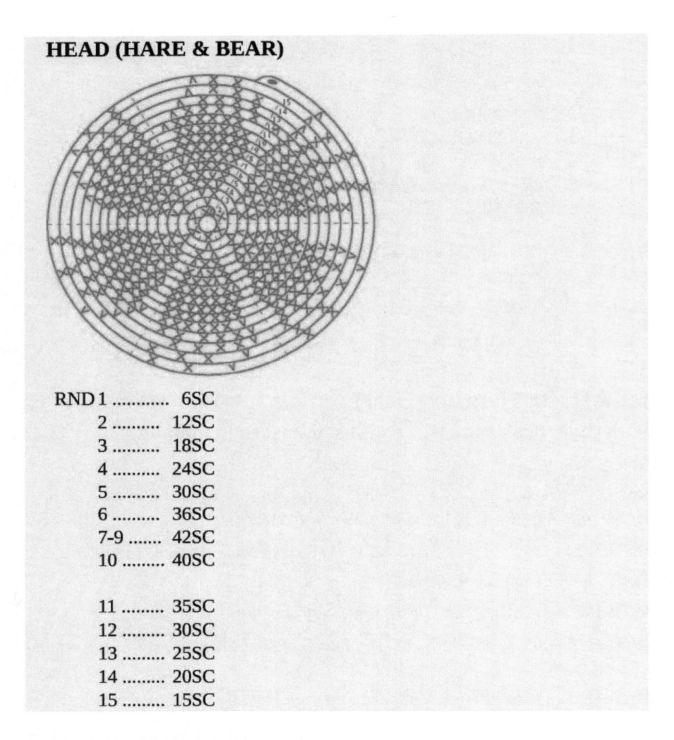

RND 1 .... 6SC
   2 .... 12SC
   3 .... 18SC
   4 .... 24SC
   5 .... 30SC
   6 .... 36SC
  7-9 .... 42SC
  10 .... 40SC

  11 .... 35SC
  12 .... 30SC
  13 .... 25SC
  14 .... 20SC
  15 .... 15SC

LEGS AND ARMS (make 4 each for Hare and Bear)

With larger hook and CC, ch 4, sl st in first ch to form ring.

RND 1: Ch 1, 6 sc into ring, place marker in last st to mark end of rnd. Do not join in first st—6 sc total.

RND 2: Work 2 sc in each st around, replace marker in last st throughout pattern —12 sc total.

RND 3: Switch to smaller hook, *sc in each of next 2 sts, dec; rep from* around—9 sc total.

RND 4: Switch to larger hook and MC, sc in each st around.

RNDS 5–22: Sc in each st around.

Sl st in next st. Fasten off, leaving a long tail for sewing.

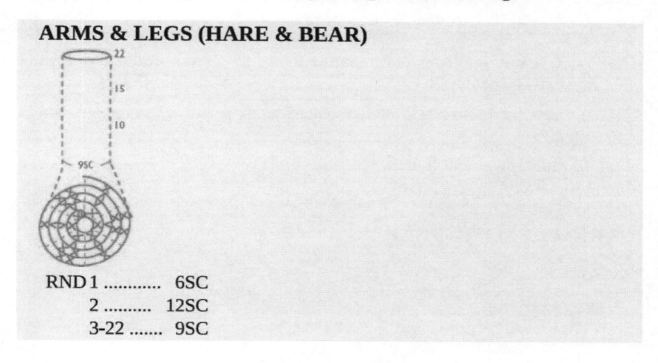

ARMS & LEGS (HARE & BEAR)

RND 1	6SC
2	12SC
3-22	9SC

EARS (make 2 for Bear)

With larger hook and CC, ch 4, sl st in first ch to form ring.

RND 1: Ch 1, 6 sc into ring, place marker in last st to mark end of rnd. Do not join in first st—6 sc total.

RND 2: Work 2 sc in each st around, replace marker in last st throughout pattern —12 sc total.

RNDS 3–4: Sc in each st around.

Sl st in next st. Fasten off, leaving a long tail for sewing.

EARS (BEAR)

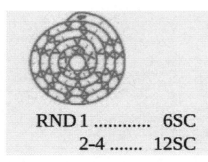

RND 1 .... 6SC

2–4 .... 12SC

AROUND NOSE (for Bear)

With larger hook and CC, ch 4, sl st in first ch to form ring.

RND 1: Ch 1, 6 sc into ring, place marker in last st to mark end of rnd. Do not join in first st—6 sc total.

RND 2: Work 2 sc in each st around, replace marker in last st throughout pattern —12 sc total.

Sl st in next st. Fasten off, leaving a long tail for sewing. Secure plastic nose to Around Nose.

AROUND NOSE (BEAR)

RND 1 .... 6SC

2 .... 12SC

EARS (make 2 for Hare)

With larger hook and MC, ch 4, sl st in first ch to form ring.

RND 1: Work 8 sc into ring, place marker in last st to mark end of rnd. Do not join in first st—8 sc total.

RNDS 2–12: Sc in each st around, replace marker in last st throughout pattern.

Sl st in next st. Fasten off, leaving a long tail for sewing.

EARS (HARE)

RND 1-12 .... 8SC

bunny

in a dress

This bunny is a little lady in her sweet dress. The spherical crochet technique for the Amigurumi makes the design look seamless and nearly machine-made. I suggest using a smaller crochet hook when decreasing the stitches to help her keep her stuffing.

yarn

1 skein Lion Brand Jiffy (100% acrylic, 135 yds ea) in color #101 Pastel Pink (MC) 1 skein Lion Brand Wool-Ease (acrylic/wool/rayon blend, 197 yds ea) in color #501 White Frost (CC1) 1 skein Bernat Softee Baby (100% acrylic, 455 yds ea) in color #205 Prettiest Pink (CC2)

hooks and notions

size F/5 (3.75mm) hook

size D/3 (3.25mm) hook

If necessary, change hook size to obtain gauge.

stitch marker

yarn needle

100% polyester fiberfill

1 pair 15mm red/pink crystal plastic eyes (Suzusei)

8mm plastic nose (Darice)

2 buttons

gauge

15 sc x 11 rows = 4" (10cm) with larger hook

finished size

8" (20cm) tall, not including ears

notes

See <u>Special Notes</u> for information on working in the round and decreasing.

HEAD

With MC and larger hook, ch 4, sl st in first ch to form ring.

RND 1: Ch 1, 8 sc into ring, place marker in last st to mark end of rnd. Do not join in first st—8 sc total.

RND 2: Work 2 sc in each st around, replace marker in last st throughout pattern —16 sc total.

RND 3: *Sc in next st, 2 sc in next st; rep from* around— 24 sc total.

RND 4: *Sc in each of next 2 sts, 2 sc in next st; rep from* around—32 sc total.

RND 5: Sc in each st around.

RND 6: *Sc in each of next 3 sts, 2 sc in next st; rep from* around—40 sc total.

RND 7: Rep Rnd 5.

RND 8: *Sc in each of next 4 sts, 2 sc in next st, sc in each of next 5 sts; rep from* around—44 sc total.

RNDS 9–13: Rep Rnd 5.

RND 14: Switch to smaller hook, *sc in each of next 2 sts, dec; rep from* around—33 sc total.

RND 15: Rep Rnd 5.

RND 16: *Sc in next st, dec; rep from* around—22 sc total.

Sl st in next st. Fasten off, leaving a long tail for sewing.

HEAD

RND 1 .... 8SC
      2 .... 16SC
      3 .... 24SC
      4-5 .... 32SC

```
6-7 ........ 40SC
8-13 ..... 44SC
14-15 .... 33SC
16 ......... 22SC
```

BODY

With MC and larger hook, ch 4, sl st in first ch to form ring.

RND 1: Ch 1, 7 sc into ring, place marker in last st to mark end of rnd. Do not join in first st—7 sc total.

RND 2: Work 2 sc in each st around, replace marker in last st throughout pattern —14 sc total.

RND 3: *Sc in next st, 2 sc in next st; rep from* around—21 sc total.

RND 4: *Sc in each of next 6 sts, 2 sc in next st; rep from* around—24 sc total.

RNDS 5–11: Sc in each st around.

RND 12: Sc in each of next 5 sts, dec, sc in each of next 10 sts, dec, sc in each st to end of rnd—22 sc total.

RND 13: Dec, sc in each of next 9 sts, dec, sc in each st to end of rnd—20 sc total.

RND 14: Rep Rnd 5.

RND 15: Sc in each of next 2 sts, dec, *sc in each of next 5 sts, dec; rep from* once, sc in each of last 2 sts—17 sc total.

Sl st in next st. Fasten off and weave in ends.

BODY

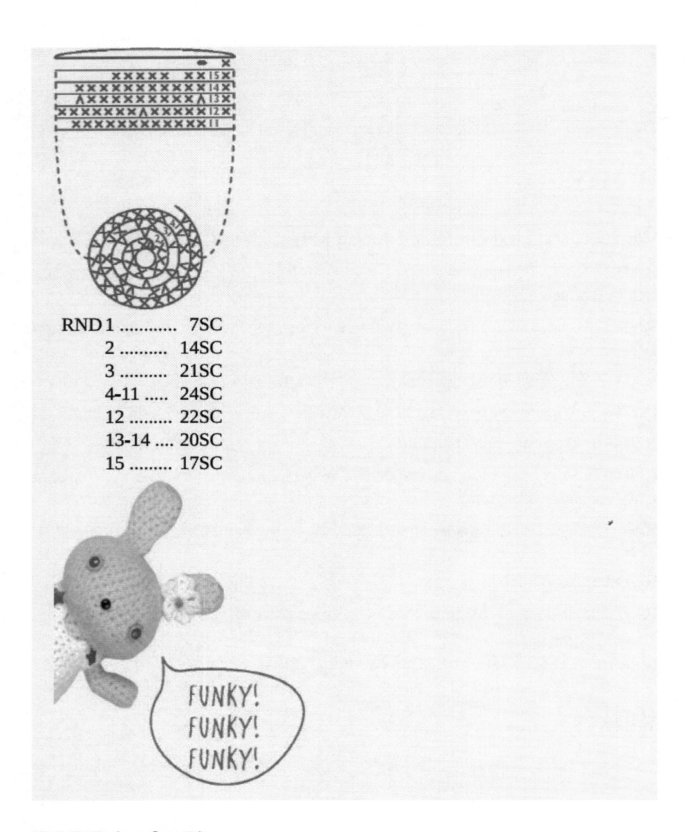

RND 1 .... 7SC
2 .... 14SC
3 .... 21SC
4-11 ..... 24SC
12 .... 22SC
13-14 .... 20SC
15 .... 17SC

EARS (make 2)

With MC and larger hook, ch 4, sl st in first ch to form ring.

RND 1: Ch 1, 6 sc into ring, place marker in last st to mark end of rnd. Do not join in first st—6 sc total.

RND 2: Work 2 sc in each st around, replace marker in last st throughout pattern —12 sc total.

RNDS 3–4: Sc in each st around.

RND 5: Dec, sc in each st around—11 sc total.

RND 6: Sc in each of next 3 sts, dec, sc in each st around—10 sc total.

RND 7: Sc in each of next 6 sts, dec, sc in each of last 2 sts—9 sc total.

RNDS 8–10: Rep Rnd 3.

Sl st in next st. Fasten off, leaving a long tail for sewing.

EARS

RND 1 .... 6SC
    2-4 .... 12SC
    5 .... 11SC
    6 .... 10SC
    7-10 .... 9SC

ARMS (make 2)

With MC and larger hook, ch 4, sl st in first ch to form ring.

RND 1: Ch 1, 5 sc into ring, place marker in last st to mark end of rnd. Do not join in first st—5 sc total.

RND 2: Work 2 sc in each st around, replace marker in last st throughout pattern —10 sc total.

RNDS 3–5: Sc in each st around.

RND 6: Sc in each of next 2 sts, dec, sc in each of next 6 sts—9 sc total.

RNDS 7–11: Rep Rnd 3.

Sl st in next st. Fasten off, leaving a long tail for sewing.

ARMS

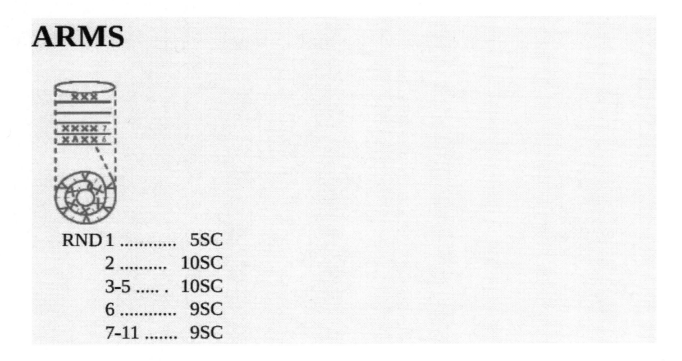

RND 1 .... 5SC
2 .... 10SC
3-5 .... 10SC
6 .... 9SC
7-11 .... 9SC

LEGS (make 2)

With MC and larger hook, ch 4, sl st in first ch to form ring.

RND 1: Ch 1, 6 sc into ring, place marker in last st to mark end of rnd. Do not join in first st—6 sc total.

RND 2: Work 2 sc in each of next 3 sts, sc in next st, 2 sc in each of next 2 sts, replace marker in last st throughout pattern—11 sc total.

RNDS 3–5: Sc in each st around.

RND 6: Dec, sc in each st around—10 sc total.

RND 7: Sc in each of next 4 sts, dec, sc in each of next 4 sts—9 sc total.

RNDS 8–9: Rep Rnd 3.

Sl st in next st. Fasten off, leaving a long tail for sewing.

LEGS

RND 1 .... 6SC

2-5 .... 11SC

6 .... 10SC

7-9 .... 9SC

DRESS

With smaller hook and CC1, ch 40. Taking care not to twist chain, sl st in first ch to form ring.

RND 1: Ch 2 (counts as hdc), hdc in each st around, sl st in 3rd ch of beg ch-3 to join—40 hdc total.

RND 2: Ch 2 (counts as hdc), hdc in each of next 5 sts, dec, *hdc in each of next 6 sts, dec; rep from* around, sl st in 3rd ch of beg ch-3 to join—35 hdc total.

RND 3: Ch 3 (counts as hdc), hdc in each st around, sl st in 3rd ch of beg ch-3 to join.

RND 4: Ch 3 (counts as hdc), dc in each of next 2 sts, dec, *hdc in each of next 5 sts, dec; rep from* around, ending hdc in each of last 2 sts, sl st in 3rd ch of beg ch-3 to join—30 hdc total.

RNDS 5–6: Ch 1, sc in each st around, sl st in first sc to join.

Front Left Side

ROW 1: Ch 1, sc in first st and in each of next 4 sts, turn— 5 sc total.

ROW 2: Ch 1, sc in each of first 4 sts, turn—4 sc total.

ROW 3: Ch 1, sc in each of first 3 sts, turn—3 sc total.

ROW 4: Ch 1, sc in each of first 2 sts, turn—2 sc total.

ROW 5: Ch 1, sc in first st, sl st in next st.
Ch 35 to make tie. Fasten off.

Front Right Side

Skip 3 sts from the last st on Row 1 of Front Left Side, attach yarn in next st. Work as for Front Left Side.

Hem

Working along bottom edge of dress, attach CC2 in any st.

ROW 1: Ch 3 (counts as dc), dc in same st, 2 dc in next st, 3 dc in next st, *2 dc in each of next 2 sts, 3 dc in next st; rep from* around, sl st in 3rd ch of beg ch-3 to join. Fasten off and weave in ends.

DRESS

CHAIN 40

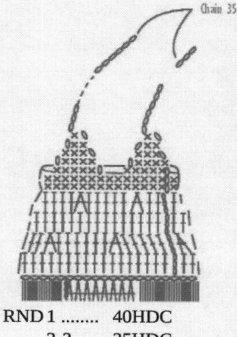

Chain 35

RND 1 .... 40HDC

2-3 ..... 35HDC

4 .... 30HDC

5-6 .... 30SC

Assembly

Stuff all the parts except the Ears with fiberfill, using only a small amount of stuffing for the Arms and Legs. Secure the eyes and nose to the Head. Use tail ends and a yarn needle to sew Ears to the Head. Use tail ends to sew the Head, Arms and Legs to the Body. Sew buttons to the Front Left and Front Right Sides of the Dress. Weave in any loose ends, and dress your bunny.

snazzy stripes

snake

This snake pattern is designed with sharp eyes and snazzy stripes. My favorite part is that you get to use turkey loop stitches on the mouth and French knots for the nose. You can wear him as a scarf during Halloween or whenever you want to keep the rats at bay.

yarn

1 skein Bernat Berella 4 (100% acrylic, 195 yds ea) in color #8722 Country Blue (MC)

1 skein Bernat Berella 4 (100% acrylic, 195 yds ea) in color #8720 Light Country Blue (CC)

scrap of Bernat Berella 4 (100% acrylic) in color #8929 Geranium (for Mouth)

hooks and notions

size F/5 (3.75mm) hook
If necessary, change hook size to obtain gauge.

100% polyester fiberfill

1 pair 12mm blue cat eyes (Suzusei)

stitch marker

yarn needle

gauge

16 sc x 8½ rows = 4" (10cm)

finished size

43" (110cm) long

notes

See Special Notes for information on working in the round and decreasing.

HEAD

With MC, ch 3, sl st in first ch to form ring.

RND 1: Work 6 sc into ring, place marker in last st to mark end of rnd. Do not join in first st—6 sc total.

RND 2: Work 2 sc in each st around, replace marker in last st throughout pattern —12 sc total.

RND 3: *Sc in next st, 2 sc in next st; rep from* around—18 sc total.

RND 4: Sc in each st around.

RND 5: *2 sc in next st, sc in each of next 2 sts; rep from* around—24 sc total.

RND 6: Sc in next st, 2 sc in next st, *sc in each of next 3 sts, 2 sc in next st; rep from* 4 times, sc in last st of rnd—30 sc total.

RND 7: Rep Rnd 4.

RND 8: *2 sc in next st, sc in each of next 4 sts; rep from* around—36 sc total.

RND 9: Sc in each of next 3 sts, 2 sc in next st, *sc in each of next 3 sts, 2 sc in next st; rep from* 4 times, sc in last st of rnd—42 sc total.

RND 10: Rep Rnd 4.

RND 11: *Sc in each of next 6 sts, 2 sc in next st; rep from* around—48 sc total.

RND 12: Sc in each of next 2 sts, 2 sc in next st, *sc in each of next 7 sts, 2 sc in next st; rep from* 4 times, sc in last st of rnd—54 sc total.

RNDS 13–20: Rep Rnd 4.

RND 21: *Sc in each of next 7 sts, dec; rep from* around—48 sc total.

RND 22: Rep Rnd 4.

RND 23: *Sc in each of next 5 sts, dec; rep from* around, ending sc in each of last 6 sts—42 sc total.

RNDS 24–31: Rep Rnd 4.

Fasten off, leaving a long tail for sewing.

HEAD

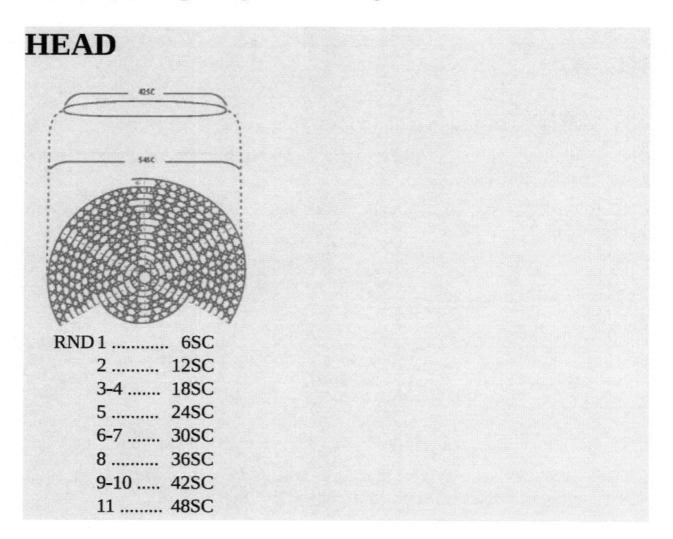

RND 1	6SC
2	12SC
3-4	18SC
5	24SC
6-7	30SC
8	36SC
9-10	42SC
11	48SC

```
12-20 .... 54SC
21-22 .... 48SC
23-31 .... 42SC
```

BODY

The Body is worked in stripes alternating seven rows of MC with seven rows of CC, ending with five MC rows. With MC, ch 3, sl st in first ch to form ring.

RND 1: Work 4 sc into ring, place marker in last st to mark end of rnd. Do not join in first st—4 sc total.

RND 2: Work 2 sc in each st around, replace marker in last st throughout pattern —8 sc total.

RND 3: Sc in each st around.

RNDS 4–7: Rep Rnd 3.

RND 8: Work 2 sc in next st, sc in each st around—9 sc total.

RNDS 9–12: Rep Rnd 3.

RND 13: Sc in each of next 2 sts, 2 sc in next st, sc in each st around—10 sc total.

RNDS 14–17: Rep Rnd 3.

RND 18: Sc in each of next 4 sts, 2 sc in next st, sc in each st around—11 sc total.

RNDS 19–22: Rep Rnd 3.

RND 23: Sc in each of next 6 sts, 2 sc in next st, sc in each st around—12 sc total.

RNDS 24–27: Rep Rnd 3.

RND 28: Sc in each of next 8 sts, 2 sc in next st, sc in each st around—13 sc total.

RNDS 29–32: Rep Rnd 3.

RND 33: Sc in each of next 10 sts, 2 sc in next st, sc in each st around—14 sc total.

RNDS 34–37: Rep Rnd 3.

RND 38: Sc in each of next 12 sts, 2 sc in next st, sc in each st around—15 sc total.

RNDS 39–42: Rep Rnd 3.

RND 43: Sc in each of next 14 sts, 2 sc in next st, sc in each st around—16 sc total.

RNDS 44–47: Rep Rnd 3.

RND 48: Sc in next st, 2 sc in next st, sc in each st around— 17 sc total.

RNDS 49–52: Rep Rnd 3.

RND 53: Sc in each of next 3 sts, 2 sc in next st, sc in each st around—18 sc total.

RNDS 54–57: Rep Rnd 3.

RND 58: Sc in each of next 5 sts, 2 sc in next st, sc in each st around—19 sc total.

RNDS 59–62: Rep Rnd 3.

RND 63: Sc in each of next 7 sts, 2 sc in next st, sc in each st around—20 sc total.

RNDS 64–67: Rep Rnd 3.

RND 68: Sc in each of next 9 sts, 2 sc in next st, sc in each st around—21 sc total.

RNDS 69–72: Rep Rnd 3.

RND 73: Sc in each of next 11 sts, 2 sc in next st, sc in each st around—22 sc total.

RNDS 74–77: Rep Rnd 3.

RND 78: Sc in each of next 13 sts, 2 sc in next st, sc in each st around—23 sc total.

RNDS 79–82: Rep Rnd 3.

RND 83: Sc in each of next 15 sts, 2 sc in next st, sc in each st around—24 sc total.

RNDS 84–87: Rep Rnd 3.

RND 88: Sc in each of next 17 sts, 2 sc in next st, sc in each st around—25 sc total.

RNDS 89–92: Rep Rnd 3.

RND 93: Sc in each of next 19 sts, 2 sc in next st, sc in each st around—26 sc total.

RNDS 94–97: Rep Rnd 3.

RND 98: Sc in each of next 21 sts, 2 sc in next st, sc in each st around—27 sc total.

RNDS 99–102: Rep Rnd 3.

RND 103: Sc in each of next 23 sts, 2 sc in next st, sc in each st around—28 sc total.

RNDS 104–107: Rep Rnd 3.

RND 108: Sc in each of next 25 sts, 2 sc in next st, sc in each st around—29 sc total.

RNDS 109–112: Rep Rnd 3.

RND 113: Sc in each of next 27 sts, 2 sc in next st, sc in each st around—30 sc total.

RNDS 114–118: Rep Rnd 3.

RND 119: Sc in each st around to last 2 sts, 2 sc in next st, sc in last st—31 sc total.

RNDS 120–124: Rep Rnd 3.

RND 125: Rep Rnd 8—32 sc total.

RNDS 126–173: Rep Rnd 3.

Fasten off, leaving a long tail for sewing.

BODY

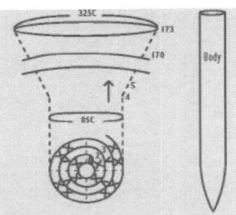

RND 1 .... 4SC
2-7 .... 8SC
8-12 .... 9SC
13-17 .... 10SC
18-22 .... 11SC
23-27 .... 12SC
28-32 .... 13SC
33-37 .... 14SC
38-42 .... 15SC
43-47 .... 16SC
48-52 .... 17SC
53-57 .... 18SC
58-62 .... 19SC
63-67 .... 20SC
68-72 .... 21SC
73-77 .... 22SC
78-82 .... 23SC
83-87 .... 24SC
88-92 .... 25SC
93-97 .... 26SC
98-102 ..... 27SC
103-107 ... 28SC
108-112 ... 29SC
113-118 ... 30SC
119-124 ... 31SC
125 .... 32SC
126-173... .32SC

ASSEMBLY

Secure the eyes to the Head. Make two French knots on the Head with a scrap of CC for the nose. Stitch a line of turkey loop stitches with Geranium yarn and a yarn needle to make the mouth. Stuff the Head with polyester fiberfill. Thread a yarn needle onto a long tail end, and sew the Head to the Body. Weave in any loose ends.

Head

stuff Snake's Head

on-the-go

water bottle carrier

Accessorize your water bottle with this cute bear. This carrier is great for when you're on-the-go with l'eau and don't want the chilly condensation sogging you up. I like google eyes, but you can use buttons or felt for eyes and make this bear happy at the gym, picnic, local fairgrounds or even riding the metro.

yarn

1 skein Lily Sugar 'N Cream (100% cotton, 120 yds ea) in color #1742 Hot Blue (MC)

1 skein Bernat Cottontots (100% cotton, 171 yds ea) in color #7 Sweet Cream (CC)

hooks and notions

size F/5 (3.75mm) hook

If necessary, change hook size to obtain gauge.

stitch marker

yarn needle

2 buttons

1 pair 15mm black moving eyes (Suzusei)

15mm black triangular plastic nose

gauge

17 sc x 10 rows = 4" (10cm)

finished size

7½" (19cm) tall, not including strap

notes

See Special Notes for information on working in the round and decreasing.

BODY

With MC, ch 4, sl st in first ch to form ring.

RND 1: Ch 1, 6 sc into ring, place marker in last st to mark end of rnd. Do not join in first st—6 sc total.

RND 2: Work 2 sc in each st around, replace marker in last st throughout pattern —12 sc total.

RND 3: *Sc in next st, 2 sc in next st; rep from* around— 18 sc total.

RND 4: *Sc in each of next 2 sts, 2 sc in next st; rep from* around—24 sc total.

RND 5: *Sc in each of next 3 sts, 2 sc in next st; rep from* around—30 sc total.

RND 6: *Sc in each of next 4 sts, 2 sc in next st; rep from* around—36 sc total.

RNDS 7–29: Sc in each st around.

Split at Back of Carrier

The following rows form the split at the back of the carrier.

ROWS 30–34: Turn, ch 1, sc in each st around.

ROW 35: Turn, ch 1, *sc in each of next 4 sts, dec; rep from* around—30 sc total.

ROW 36: Turn, ch 1, sc in each st around.

ROW 37: Turn, ch 1, *sc in each of next 3 sts, dec; rep from* around—24 sc total.

ROWS 38–39: Turn, ch 1, sc in each st around.

Fasten off, leaving a long tail.

BODY

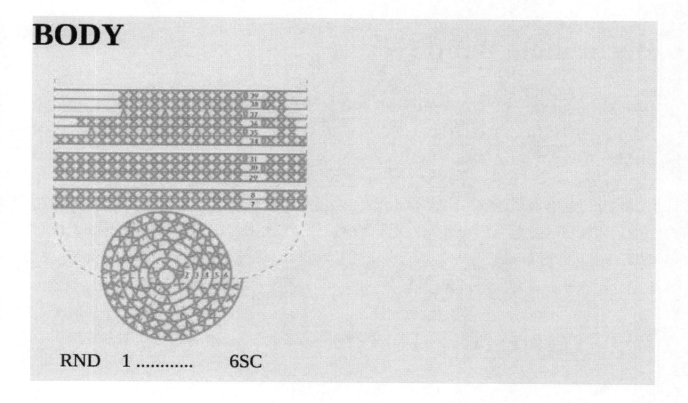

RND 1 .... 6SC

2	12SC
3	18SC
4	24SC
5	30SC
6-29	36SC
BEGIN WORKING FLAT	
ROW 30-34	36SC
35-36	30SC
37-39	24SC

Buttonhole Band

Working along the row ends on the left side of the split, attach MC in the upper right corner. Ch 1, sc in end of first row, sc in end of each of next 4 rows, ch 5, counting backwards, skip previous 3 sc, sl st in next sc. Work 7 sc into ch-5 sp. Continuing across row ends, work 5 sc evenly across next 4 row ends, ch 5, counting backwards, skip previous 3 sc, sl st in next sc. Work 7 sc into ch-5 sp. Sc in last row end.

Fasten off and weave in ends.

BUTTONHOLE BAND

EARS (make 2)

With CC, ch 4, sl st in first ch to form ring.

RND 1: Ch 1, 8 sc into ring, place marker in last st to mark end of rnd. Do not join in first st—8 sc total.

RND 2: Sc in each st around.

RND 3: Sc in each st around to last st, sl st in last st.
Fasten off, leaving a long tail for sewing.

STRAP

With MC, leave a long tail for sewing, then ch 126.

ROW 1: Sc in second ch from hook and in each ch across— 125 sc total.

ROW 2: Turn, ch 1, sc in each st across.
Fasten off, leaving a long tail for sewing.

AROUND NOSE

With CC, work as for Ears. Secure plastic nose to center of Around Nose.

AROUND NOSE & EARS

STRAP

Assembly

Sew the Strap to the Body securely 1" to 2" (3cm to 5cm) from the top edge of the bag on opposite sides. Use tail ends and a yarn needle to sew the Ears and Nose to the bag. Secure the eyes to the bag as well. Using the buttonholes as a guide, sew the buttons onto the right side of the split on the back of the bag. Weave in any loose ends.

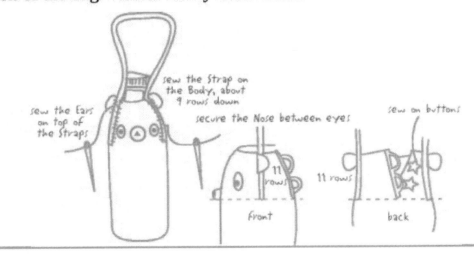

Super-Cool Accessories

This chapter will show you how to make whimsical accessories that accent your favorite outfits and even keep you warm on a cold day. Many of the pieces in this chapter use basic stitches such as single, half-double, double, triple crochet and cluster stitches. Even if you don't know what these stitches mean right off the bat, you can find instructions in a great many "How-To" crochet books for beginners, and you can even take classes at your local community college or yarn store. If you'd like to start off with an easier project, I'd suggest you try the **Bouclé Skull Cap with Glitter Edge** , the **Lazy Daze E-Z Hat** or the **Flower Scarf**. The most challenging designs are the **Luscious Blues Flower Scarf** and the **Puffy Flowers Scarf**. If you need to whip up a quick fashion accent, try the **Spring Chicks and Baby Bunnies Corsage**, **Geometric Earrings** or the **Striped Wristband**. And, if you're on a long plane trip to Paris or Mongolia, you may have enough time to crochet the **Scarf Hoodie**.

These designs are popular among all sorts of people, so don't be shy. Once you've learned the basic pattern, you can make your own unique designs by just changing colors and using different materials. Hey, your mother, daughter, grandmother and granddaughter might just like it! I'm delighted to share these designs with you.

**bouclé skull cap with
glitter edge**

This hat is made with bouclé yarn and glitter yarn. Bouclé yarn is thick, bulky and very soft, which makes this project go quickly. Finishing the edge with glitter yarn makes this hat distinctive and a little spunky.

yarn

2 skeins Lion Brand Lion Bouclé (acrylic/mohair/ nylon blend, 57 yds ea) in color #213 Taffy (MC) 1 skein Patons Brilliant (acrylic/nylon/polyester blend, 166 yds ea) in color #23 Gold Glow (CC)

hooks and notions

size I/9 (5.5mm) hook

If necessary, change hook size to obtain gauge.

yarn needle

gauge

11 dc x 4 rows = 4" (10cm)

finished size

19" (48cm) around x 7½" (19cm) tall

notes

Please refer to the individual patterns for instructions on which rounds should be joined.

HAT

With MC, ch 4, sl st in first ch to form ring.

RND 1: Ch 3 (counts as first dc), work 12 dc into ring, place marker in last st to mark end of rnd. Do not join in first st—13 dc total.

RND 2: Work 2 dc in each st around, replace marker in last st throughout pattern —26 dc total.

RND 3: *Dc in next st, 2 dc in next st; rep from* around— 39 dc total.

RNDS 4–6: Dc in each st around.

RND 7: Work *2 dc in next st, dc in each of next 11 sts; rep from* twice, 2 dc in next st, dc in each of last 2 sts—43 dc total.

RNDS 8–10: Dc in each st around.

Sl st in next st. Fasten off, leaving a long tail.

RND 11: Beg 10 sts from last st worked, join CC, ch 1, work 2 sc in each dc around, sl st in first sc to join—86 sc total.

RNDS 12–13: Ch 1, sc in each st around.

Sl st in next st. Fasten off, leaving a long tail. Use a yarn needle to weave in ends.

HAT

```
RND 1 .......... 13DC
     2 .......... 26DC
     3-6 ....... 39DC
     7-10 ..... 43DC
     11-13 .... 86SC
```

sporty hat

with a brim

The technique for this pattern is more intricate because of the addition of the brim. Not only will it help keep the sun out of your eyes, but you can customize it by putting a team's insignia on the front for your favorite sports fan.

yarn

2 skeins Lion Brand Wool-Ease (acrylic/wool/rayon blend, 197 yds ea) in color #112 Red Sprinkles

hooks and notions

size I/9 (5.5mm) hook

If necessary, change hook size to obtain gauge.

stitch marker

yarn needle

gauge

12 hdc x 5 rows = 4" (10cm) with 2 strands held together

finished size

19" (48cm) around x 8¼" (21cm) tall, including brim

notes

This pattern is worked in the round without joining. Place a marker in the last stitch of each round to mark the end of the round. Do not turn at the end of each round.

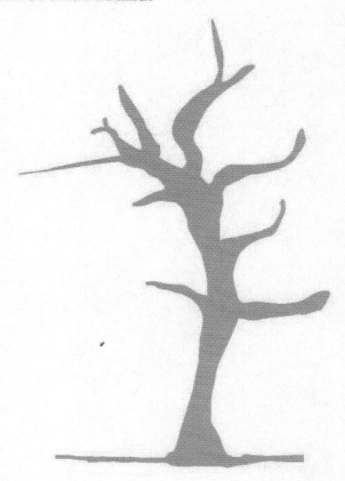

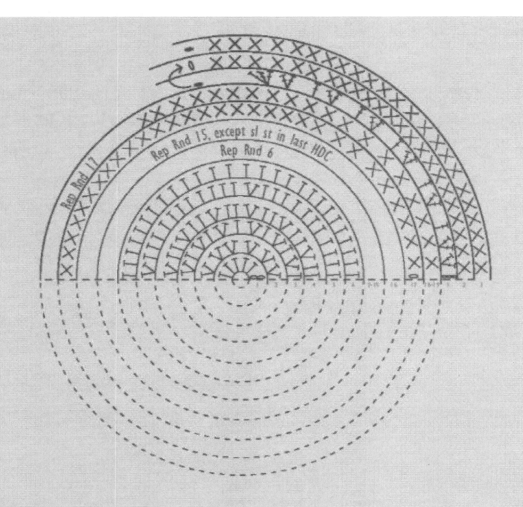

Rep Rnd 17
Rep Rnd 15, except sl st in last HDC
Rep Rnd 6

HAT

RND 1 .... 13HDC
2 .... 26HDC
3 .... 39HDC
4 .... 52HDC
5-16 ... 56HDC
17-19 .... 56SC

BRIM

RND 1 .... 23DC
2-3 .... 23SC

HAT

With 2 strands of yarn held tog, ch 4, sl st in first ch to form ring.

RND 1: Ch 2 (counts as first hdc), work 12 hdc into ring, place marker in last st to mark end of rnd. Do not join in first st—13 hdc total.

RND 2: Work 2 hdc in each st around, replace marker in last st throughout pattern—26 hdc total.

RND 3: *Hdc in next st, 2 hdc in next st; rep from* around—39 hdc total.

RND 4: *Hdc in each of next 2 sts, 2 hdc in next st; rep from* around—52 hdc total.

RND 5: *Hdc in each of next 11 sts, 2 hdc in next st; rep from* 3 times, hdc in each of last 4 sts—56 hdc total.

RNDS 6–15: Hdc in each st around.

RND 16: Hdc in each st to last hdc, sl st in last hdc.

RNDS 17–19: Ch 1, sc in each st around, sl st in first sc to join.

BRIM

RND 1: Ch 3 (counts as first dc), 2 dc in each of next 2 sts, *dc in next st, 2 dc in next st; rep from* 4 times, 3 dc in next st, skip next 2 sts, sl st in next st, turn—23 dc total.

RND 2: Ch 1, sc in each dc across, skip next 2 sts from Rnd 19, sl st in next st, turn—23 sc total.

RND 3: Ch 1, sc in each sc across brim, sl st in beg ch-1.

Fasten off, leaving a long tail. Use a yarn needle to weave in ends.

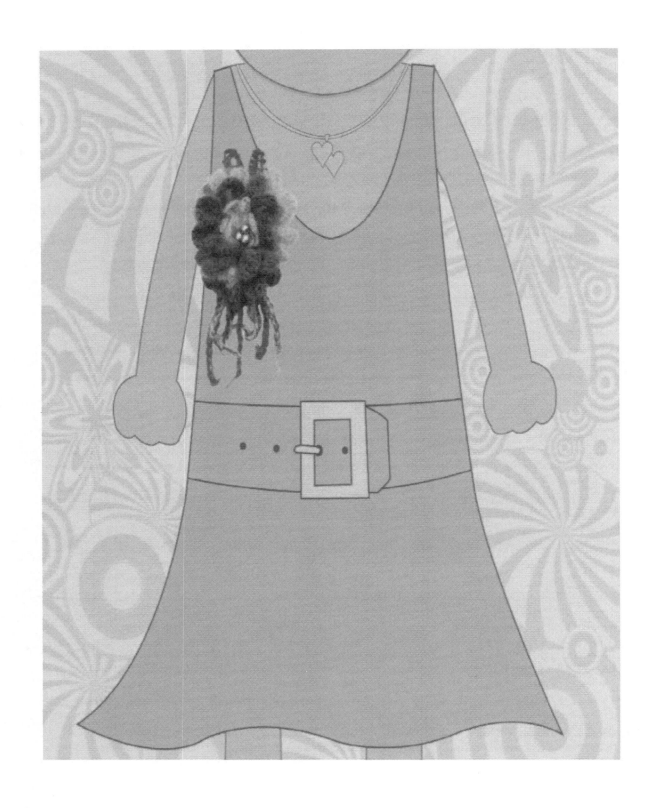

spring chicks and baby

bunnies corsage

The corsage is a fun accent to any outfit. I like to use different yarns and colors to create my own daily bouquet of wearable flowers. The pearls in the center and the mohair yarn on my pattern remind me of spring chicks and baby bunnies.

yarn

1 skein Crystal Palace Yarns Kid Merino (kid mohair/ merino wool/micro nylon blend, 240 yds ea) in color #4686 Strawberry Soda (MC) 1 skein Crystal Palace Yarns Kid Merino (kid mohair/ merino wool/micro nylon blend, 240 yds ea) in color #4672 Berry (CC1) 1 skein Crystal Palace Yarns Kid Merino (kid mohair/ merino wool/micro nylon blend, 240 yds ea) in color #4676 Pacific Blue (CC2)

hooks and notions

size C/2 (2.75mm) hook

If necessary, change hook size to obtain gauge.

yarn needle

25–35 6mm glass beads (Gutermann)

nylon beading thread

pin back

gauge

23 sc x 38 rows = 4" (10cm)

finished size

Large Flower

2" (5cm) in diameter

Small Flower

1½" (4cm) in diameter

Leaf

2" (5cm) in diameter

SMALL FLOWER (make 4: 2 small flowers with MC and 2 small flowers with CC1) With MC (or CC1) and leaving a 16" (41cm) tail, ch 4, sl st in first ch to form ring.

RND 1: Work (ch 10, sl st into ring) 8 times.

Fasten off, leaving a 16" (41cm) tail.

SMALL FLOWER (MAKE 4)

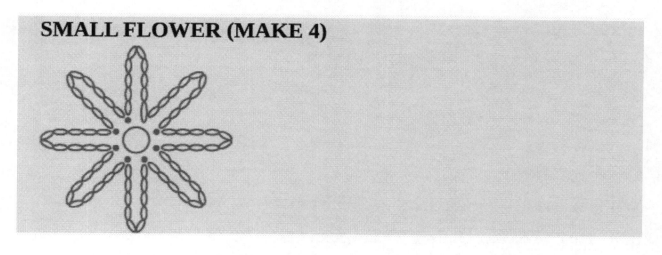

LARGE FLOWER (make 4: 2 large flowers with MC and 2 large flowers with CC1) With MC (or CC1) and leaving a 16" (41cm) tail, ch 4, sl st in first ch to form ring.

RND 1: Ch 1, work 8 sc into ring, sl st in first sc to join.

RND 2: Work (ch 10, sl st in next sc) 8 times.

RND 3: *Work (ch 1, 2 sc, 2 hdc, 6 dc, 2 hdc, 2 sc, ch 1) in next ch-10 sp, sl st in next sl st; rep from* 7 more times, sl st in beg ch-1 to join.

Fasten off, leaving a 16" (41cm) tail.

LARGE FLOWER (MAKE 4)

LEAF (make 3)

With CC2 and leaving a 16" (41cm) tail, ch 12.

RND 1: Sc in second ch from hook, hdc in next st, dc in each of next 2 sts, trc in next st, dc in each of next 2 sts, hdc in each of next 2 sts, sc in each of next 2 sts, working around the bottom of the ch, sc in each of next 2 sts, hdc in each of next 2 sts, dc in each of next 2 sts, trc in next st, dc in each of next 2 sts, hdc in next st, sc in next st, sl st in skipped ch at beg of rnd—22 sts total.

Fasten off, leaving a 16" (41cm) tail.

LEAF (MAKE 3)

Assembly

Place one Small Flower on top of one Large Flower, drawing all the tails through the center of the flowers and out the bottom. Repeat for the remaining three sets of flowers. Make chain stitches to the end of each tail and fasten off. Make chains for the ends of the Leaf tails and fasten off. Thread beads onto nylon beading thread and sew them to the center of each flower set. Arrange all four sets of flowers with leaves, bundling the chain tails together with a long strand of yarn. Secure a pin back with nylon beading thread to the back of the flowers, leaving the chain tails to hang below.

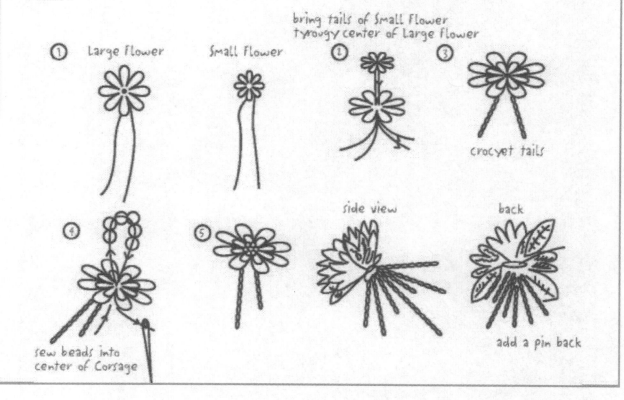

lazy daze

E-Z **hat**

This hat is great for beginners. Only single and double crochet stitches are used to make this hat. If you're an experienced crocheter, this is a good opportunity to make something fun while you are watching TV or just plain zoning out.

yarn

1 skein Lion Brand Yarn Moonlight Mohair (acrylic/mohair/cotton/metallic polyester blend, 82 yds ea) in color #207 Coral Reef

hooks and notions

size I/9 (5.5mm) hook

If necessary, change hook size to obtain gauge.

stitch marker

yarn needle

gauge

13 dc x 4½ rows = 4" (10cm)

finished size

20" (51cm) around x 8¼" (21cm) tall

notes

This pattern is worked in the round without joining. Place a marker in the last stitch of each round to mark the end of the round. Do not turn at the end of each round.

HAT

With MC, ch 4, sl st in first ch to form ring.

RND 1: Ch 3 (counts as first dc), work 12 dc into ring, place marker in last st to mark end of rnd. Do not join in first st—13 dc total.

RND 2: Work 2 dc in each st around, replace marker in last st throughout pattern —26 dc total.

RND 3: *Dc in next st, 2 dc in next st; rep from* around—39 dc total.

RND 4: *Dc in each of next 2 sts, 2 dc in next st; rep from* around—52 dc total.

RND 5: Dc in each st around.

RNDS 6–12: Rep Rnd 5.

RND 13: Dc in each st around to last st, sl st in last dc.

RND 14: Ch 1, sc in each st around, do not join in first sc—52 sc total.

RNDS 15–16: Sc in next st and in each st around.

Fasten off, leaving a long tail. Use a yarn needle to weave in ends.

HAT

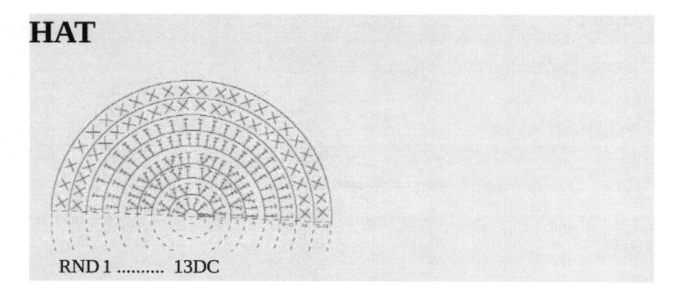

RND 1 .... 13DC

```
2 .......... 26DC
3 .......... 39DC
4-13 ..... 52DC
14-16 .... 52SC
```

your favorite you

flower bag

This bag can be for your favorite girl or for your favorite you. It's a perfect on-the-go crochet kit to hold your latest project, needles, hooks and yarn! After making each part, fold the handle in half widthwise and sew together with woven seams. It's good to make sure the handles are placed correctly.

yarn

1 skein The Leader Aran (100% acrylic, 220 yds ea) in color #124 Yellow-Orange (MC)

1 skein The Leader Aran (100% acrylic, 220 yds ea) in color #129 Orange (CC1)

1 skein The Leader Aran (100% acrylic, 220 yds ea) in color #030 Light Yellow (CC2)

hooks and notions

size F/5 (3.75mm) hook

size D/3 (3.25mm) hook

If necessary, change hook size to obtain gauge.

stitch marker

yarn needle

gauge

16 sc x 10 rows = 4" (10cm) with larger hook

finished size

7½" (19cm) wide x 7" (18cm) tall, excluding handles

Flower measures 2" (5cm) in diameter

notes

This pattern is worked in the round without joining. Place a marker in the last stitch of each round to mark the end of the round. Do not turn at the end of each round.

PURSE BODY

With larger hook and MC, ch 4, sl st in first ch to form ring.

RND 1: Ch 1, 6 sc into ring, place marker in last st to mark end of rnd. Do not join in first st—6 sc total.

RND 2: Work 2 sc in each st around, replace marker in last st throughout pattern —12 sc total.

RND 3: *Sc in next st, 2 sc in next st; rep from* around—18 sc total.

RND 4: *Sc in each of next 2 sts, 2 sc in next st; rep from* around—24 sc total.

RND 5: Sc in next st, 2 sc in next st, *sc in each of next 3 sts, 2 sc in next st; rep from* 4 times, sc in last st of rnd—30 sc total.

RND 6: *Sc in each of next 4 sts, 2 sc in next st; rep from* around—36 sc total.

RND 7: Sc in each of next 2 sts, 2 sc in next st, *sc in each of next 5 sts, 2 sc in next st; rep from* 4 times, sc in last st of rnd—42 sc total.

RND 8: *Sc in each of next 6 sts, 2 sc in next st; rep from* around—48 sc total.

RND 9: Sc in each of next 5 sts, 2 sc in next st, *sc in each of next 11 sts, 2 sc in next st; rep from* twice, sc in each of last 6 sts—52 sc total.

RNDS 10–14: Sc in each st around.

RND 15: Sc in each of first 12 sts, 2 sc in next st, sc in each of next 25 sts, 2 sc in next st, sc in each of last 13 sts—54 sc total.

RND 16: Rep Rnd 10.

RND 17: 2 sc in next st, sc in each of next 26 sts, 2 sc in next st, sc in each st around—56 sc total.

RND 18: Rep Rnd 10.

RND 19: Sc in each of next 6 sts, 2 sc in next st, sc in each of next 27 sts, 2 sc in next st, sc in each st around—58 sc total.

RND 20: Rep Rnd 10.

RND 21: Sc in each of next 21 sts, 2 sc in next st, sc in each of next 28 sts, 2 sc in next st, sc in each st around— 60 sc total.

RND 22: Rep Rnd 10.

RND 23: Sc in each of next 4 sts, 2 sc in next st, sc in each of next 39 sts, 2 sc in next st, sc in each st around—62 sc total.

RND 24: Rep Rnd 10.

RND 25: 2 sc in next st, sc in each of next 30 sts, 2 sc in next st, sc in each st around—64 sc total.

RND 26: Rep Rnd 10.

RND 27: Sc in each of next 7 sts, 2 sc in next st, sc in each of next 31 sts, 2 sc in next st, sc in each st around—66 sc total.

RND 28: Rep Rnd 10.

RND 29: Sc in each of next 24 sts, 2 sc in next st, sc in each of next 32 sts, 2 sc in next st, sc in each st around—68 sc total.

RND 30: Rep Rnd 10.

RND 31: Sc in each of next 16 sts, 2 sc in next st, sc in each of next 33 sts, 2 sc in next st, sc in each st around— 70 sc total.

RND 32: Rep Rnd 10.

RND 33: 2 sc in next st, sc in each of next 34 sts, 2 sc in next st, sc in each st around—72 sc total.

RND 34: Rep Rnd 10.

Fasten off. Use a yarn needle to weave in ends.

BODY

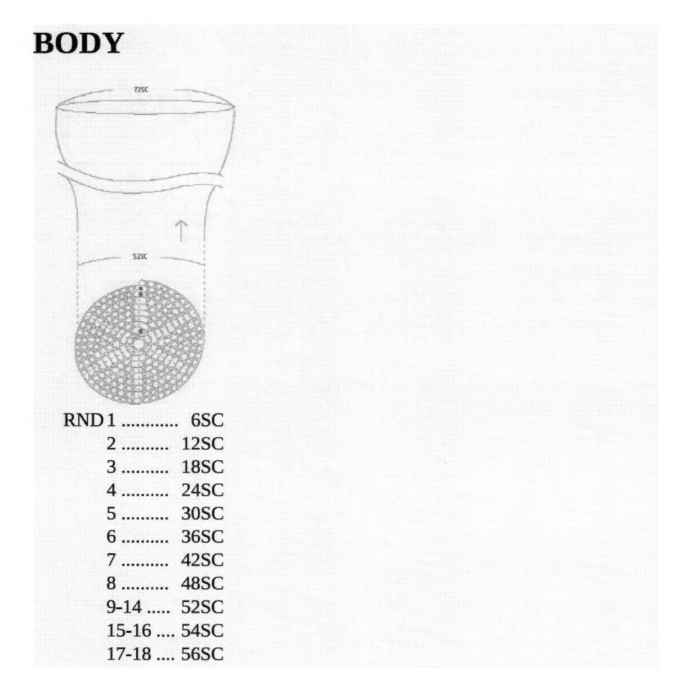

RND 1 .... 6SC
    2 .... 12SC
    3 .... 18SC
    4 .... 24SC
    5 .... 30SC
    6 .... 36SC
    7 .... 42SC
    8 .... 48SC
    9-14 ..... 52SC
    15-16 .... 54SC
    17-18 .... 56SC

```
19-20 .... 58SC
21-22 .... 60SC
23-24 .... 62SC
25-26 .... 64SC
27-28 .... 66SC
29-30 .... 68SC
31-32 .... 70SC
33-34 .... 72SC
```

HANDLES (make 2)

With larger hook and MC, ch 47.

ROW 1: Sc in second ch from hook and in each ch across, turn—46 sc total.

ROWS 2–6: Ch 1, sc in each st across, turn.

Fasten off. Use a yarn needle to weave in ends.

Fold in half widthwise and sew long edges together (see diagram at right).

HANDLE

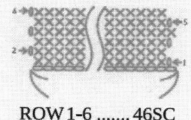

ROW 1-6 .... 46SC

FLOWER (make 4)

With smaller hook and CC1, ch 3, sl st in first ch to form ring.

RND 1: Work 6 sc into ring, sl st in first sc to join.

RND 2: Ch 1, 2 sc in each st around, sl st in first sc to join—12 sc total.
Fasten off.

RND 3: With CC2 in any st from previous rnd, * work (ch 3, 3 dc, drop loop from hook, insert hook in top of ch-3, pick up dropped loop and draw through loop on hook, ch 3, sl st) 6 times around—6 petals.

Fasten off, leaving a long tail for sewing.

FLOWER

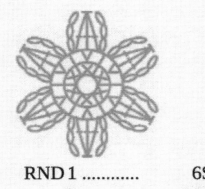

RND 1	6SC
2	12SC
3	6 PETALS

Finishing

Turn the bag inside out, and pin about 1½" (4cm) of both ends of one Handle to the inside of the bag, approximately 2" (5cm) in from each side of the bag. Sew the Handle ends to the inside of the bag with a yarn needle and MC. Repeat for the remaining Handle on the other side of the bag. Turn the bag right side out and sew a Flower over each Handle using a yarn needle and CC2 to match the center of each Flower.

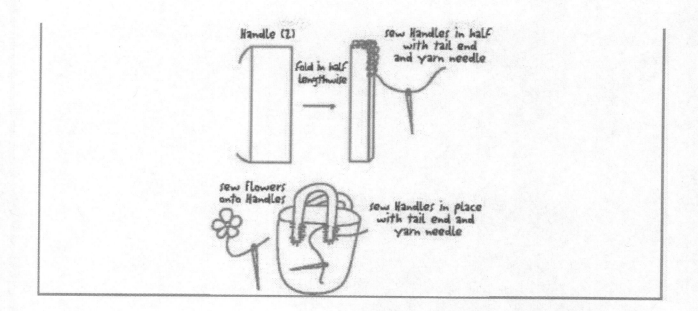

In this project, you can learn or practice how to join motifs together. It seems more complicated than it is. Just slip-stitch into the corresponding place of the adjoining motif and then work the appropriate stitches in the motif that's in progress. Rinse and repeat.

yarn

1 skein Tahki Yarns Cotton Classic (100% mercerized cotton, 108

yds ea) in color #3703 Green (MC)

1 skein Tahki Yarns Cotton Classic (100% mercerized cotton, 108 yds ea) color #3713 Meadow (CC)

hooks and notions

size F/5 (3.75mm) hook

If necessary, change hook size to obtain gauge.

yarn needle

gauge

16 sc x 15 rows = 4" (10cm)

finished size

4" (10cm) wide x 52½" (133cm) long

green tones
flower scarf

FLOWER MOTIF

FLOWER MOTIF

MOTIF (make 12)

With MC, ch 6, sl st in first ch to form ring.

RND 1: Ch 1, 12 sc into ring, sl st in first sc to join—12 sc total.

RND 2: Ch 8 (counts as dc, ch 5), *skip next st, dc in next st, ch 5; rep from* around, sl st in 3rd ch of beg ch-5 to join—6 ch-5 spaces.

RND 3: Ch 1, work (sc, hdc, 5 dc, hdc, sc) into each ch-5 sp around, sl st in beg ch-1 to join—6 petals total.

RND 4: Switch to CC, ch 1, sc in same space as sl st, *ch 6, sl st in same sc to make loop, ch 6, sk next 9 sts (1 petal), sc in sp between petals; rep from* around, sl st in first sc to join.

RND 5: Work (sc, hdc, 5 dc, hdc, sc) into first ch-6 loop, (sc, hdc, 7 dc, hdc, sc) into next ch-6 sp; rep around, sl st in first sc to join.

Assembly

Crochet each motif to the next one while crocheting Rnd 5, working in slip stitch. Follow the arrows in the diagram above to see where the slip stitches are attached to the adjacent motifs.

SPECIAL STITCHES

5-dc Cluster: Yo, insert hook in st, yo, pull through st, yo, pull through 2 lps on hook, (yo, insert hook in same st, yo, pull through st, yo, pull through 2 lps on hook) 4 times, yo, pull through all lps on hook, ch 1.

2-dc Cluster: Yo, insert hook in st, yo, pull through st, yo, pull through 2 lps on hook, yo, insert hook in same st, yo, pull through st, yo, pull through 2 lps on hook, yo, pull through all lps on hook, ch 1.

This pattern is a challenging project for a beginner. If you can get comfortable with joining motifs together, the other challenge is the delicacy of the mohair yarn. The finished product turns out to be a lovely, lightweight and luscious scarf. Definitely worth the effort.

yarn

2 skeins/balls Crystal Palace Yarns Kid Merino (kid mohair/ merino wool/micro nylon blend, 240 yds ea) in color #4676 Pacific Blue (MC)

2 skeins/balls Crystal Palace Yarns Kid Merino (kid mohair/merino wool/mictro nylon blend, 240 yds ea) in color #4681 Misty Blue (C)

hooks and notions

size D/3 (3.25mm) hook

If necessary, change hook size to obtain gauge.

yarn needle

gauge

19 sc x 33 rows = 4" (10cm)

finished size

6½" (17cm) wide x 63" (160cm) long

Each flower measures 3½" (9cm) in diameter

luscious blues
flower scarf

MOTIF A (make 14)

With MC, ch 4, sl st in first ch to form ring.

RND 1: Ch 3 (counts as first dc), 15 dc into ring, sl st in 3rd ch of beg ch-3 to join—16 dc total.

RND 2: *Ch 4, 5-dc cluster in next st, ch 4, sl st in next st; rep from* around, sl st in 1st ch of beg ch-4 to join—8 clusters total.

RND 3: Change to CC, sl st in each of next 3 ch, ch 1, *sc in top of next cluster, ch 5; rep from* around, sl st in first sc to join—8 ch-5 spaces total.

RND 4: * Ch 3, work ([2-dc cluster, ch 2] three times) in each ch-5 sp around, sl st in 3rd ch of beg ch-3 to join.

RND 5: Ch 1, * sc in next cluster, ch 5; rep from * around, sl st in beg ch-1 to join.

MOTIF B (make 14)

Work as for Motif A, reversing colors.

FLOWER MOTIF

Assembly

In the final round (Rnd 5) of each flower motif, use a slip stitch to link one motif to the next, following the arrows in the diagram to see how the motifs are linked together. You will link a total of 14 Motif A and 14 Motif B.

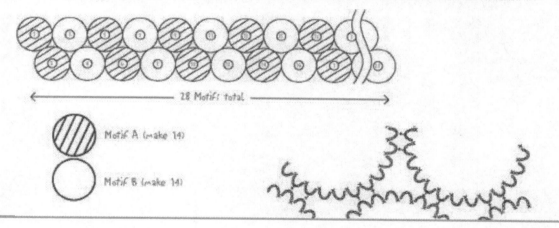

puffy flowers

scarf

This elaborate project involves more than just crocheting. After making all the lively flowers, there is an intricate design to connect them together. The flowers, chains and end motifs make this scarf delicate and charming. I know from experience the wearer feels like royalty.

yarn

2 skeins Crystal Palace Yarn Merino Frapp (80% merino/ 20% nylon, 140 yds ea) in color #143 heathered red (MC)

2 skeins Crystal Palace Yarn Merino Frapp (80% merino/ 20% nylon, 140 yds ea) in color #29B heathered mauve (CC1)

2 skeins Crystal Palace Yarn Merino Frapp (80% merino/ 20% nylon, 140 yds ea) in color #146 heathered purple (CC2)

1 skein each Crystal Palace Yarns Kid Merino (merino/ kid mohair/micro nylon blend, 240 yds ea) in color #4686 Strawberry Soda (CC3) and #4672 Berry (CC4)

hooks and notions

size F/5 (3.75mm) hook

If necessary, change hook size to obtain gauge.

yarn needle

gauge

15 sc x 12 rows = 4" (10cm) with MC

finished size

64" (163cm) long

Each flower measures 3½" (9cm) in diameter

MOTIF A (make 14)

With MC, ch 4, sl st in first ch to form ring.

RND 1: Ch 3 (counts as dc), 11 dc into ring, sl st in 3rd ch of beg ch-3 to join—12 dc total.

RND 2: Ch 6 (counts as dc, ch 3), dc in same st as join, work (dc, ch 3, dc) in each st around, sl st in 3rd ch of beg ch-6 to join—24 dc total.

RND 3: Ch 3, *3 dc in ch-3 sp, ch 3, sc in sp between next 2 dc sts, ch 3; rep from* around, sl st in 3rd ch to join—12 groups of 3 dc total.

Fasten off, leaving a long tail. Weave in all ends.

MOTIF B (make 14)

With CC1, work as for Motif A.

MOTIF C (make 14)

With CC2, work as for Motif A.

FLOWER MOTIFS A-C

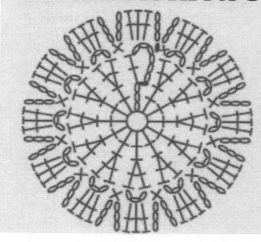

MOTIF D (make 6)

With CC3 and CC4 held together, ch 4, sl st in first ch to form ring.

RND 1: Ch 3 (counts as dc), 11 dc into ring, sl st in 3rd ch of beg ch-3 to join—12 dc total.

Do not fasten off.

FLOWER MOTIF D

Finishing

Attach CC3 in any st of one Motif D, ch 10, sc in any sc (between dc groups) of Motif A. *Ch 13, sc in sc on opposite side of same Motif A, ch 2, sc in any sc of next Motif A; rep from* until all 16 of Motif A are joined.

Ch 10, sl st in any st of second Motif D.

Join all of Motif B in one strip and all of Motif C in one strip in the same manner as Motif A.

Lay strips of A and B next to each other with WS facing. Lay strip of C with RS facing on top between A and B. Sew all three strips together. Weave in any loose ends.

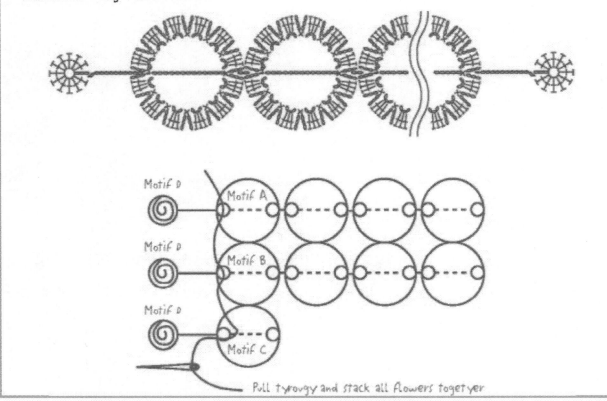

flower hat

and scarf set

This flapper-style hat can be made very easily. Make sure to leave long loose ends when you make the flower to weave it more easily onto the hat. Some fun color combinations to try are a moss green hat with an ivory flower or a chocolate hat with a pink flower. The matching scarf is made with a half-double crochet stitch all the way across. It's so simple to make, but the slip-on flower makes this scarf very original.

yarn

Hat and Scarf

3 skeins Lion Brand Wool-Ease (acrylic/wool blend, 197 yds ea) in color #153 Black (MC) *1 skein for Hat; 2 skeins for Scarf*

1 skein Red Heart Super Saver (100% acrylic, 364 yds ea) in color #378 Claret for flowers (CC)

hooks and notions

size G/6 (4.50mm) hook (for Hat)

size I/9 (5.50mm) hook (for Scarf)

size F/5 (3.75mm) hook (for Flowers)

If necessary, change hook size to obtain gauge.

yarn needle

stitch markers

gauge

Hat

15 dc and 6 rows = 4" (10cm) on size G/6 (4.50mm) hook

Scarf

12 hdc and 6 rows = 4" (10cm) on size I/9 (5.50mm) with two strands of MC held together **finished sizes**

Hat

24" (61cm) around x 9" (23cm) tall

Scarf

71" (180cm) long x 4" (10cm) wide

Flower

4" (10cm) in diameter (for Scarf & Hat)

notes

The hat pattern is worked in the round without joining. Place a marker in the last stitch of each round to mark the end of the round. Do not turn at the end of each round.

HAT

With G/6 (4.50mm) hook and MC, ch 4, sl st in first ch to form ring.

RND 1: Ch 6 (counts as dc, ch 3) *dc into ring, ch 3* ; rep between * 4 more times, do not join in beg of rnd—6 ch-3 loops total.

RND 2: Work 2 dc in 3rd ch of beg ch-6 on first row, ch 1, sk 1 ch, 2 dc in next ch, ch 1, sk 1 ch, * 2 dc in next dc, ch 1, sk 1 ch, 2 dc in next ch, ch 1, sk 1 ch, ; *rep between* 4 more times—24 dc total.

RND 3: * Dc in next st, 2 dc in next st, ch 1, sk 1 ch ; *rep between* around—36 dc total.

RND 4: * Dc in each of next 2 sts, 2 dc in next st, ch 1, sk 1 ch ; *rep between* around—48 dc total.

RND 5: * Dc in each of next 2 sts, ch 2, sk 1 dc, dc in next st, ch 1, sk 1 ch ; *rep between* around—36 dc total.

RND 6: * Dc in each of next 2 sts, ch 1, sk 1 ch, dc in next ch, dc in next dc, ch 1, sk 1 ch ; *rep between* around— 48 dc total.

RNDS 7–12: * Dc in each of next 2 sts, ch 1, sk 1 ch ; *rep between* around.

RND 13: Rep Row 12, ending sl st in first dc of rnd.

RNDS 14–16: Ch 1, sc in each st and ch around, sl st in first sc to join—72 sc.

Fasten off. Use a yarn needle to weave in tail ends.

HAT

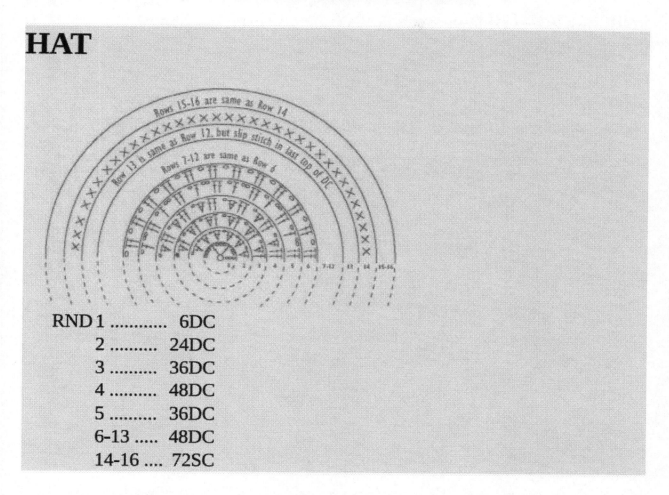

RND 1 .... 6DC

2 .... 24DC

3 .... 36DC

4 .... 48DC

5 .... 36DC

6-13 ..... 48DC

14-16 .... 72SC

FLOWER

Leave approx a 19" (48cm) tail to sew the flower onto the hat. With size F/5 (3.75mm) hook and CC, ch 4, sl st in first ch to form ring.

RND 1: Ch 5 (counts as 1 dc, ch 2), * dc into ring, ch 2 , *rep between* 4 more times, sl st in 3rd ch of beg ch-5 to join—6 ch-2 lps.

RND 2: Ch 1, work (sc, 2 hdc, dc, 2 hdc, sc) into each ch-2 sp around, sl st in first sc to join, turn (6 petals).

RND 3: (Ch 3, sl st) in between petals from previous row 5 times, ch 3, sl st in first ch of beg ch-3, turn.

RND 4: Ch 1, work (sc, 2 hdc, 3 dc, 2 hdc, sc) into each ch-3 sp around, sl st in first sc to join, turn.

RND 5: (Ch 4, sl st) in between petals from previous row 5 times, ch 3, sl st in first ch of beg ch-4, turn.

RND 6: Ch 1, work (sc, 3 hdc, 4 dc, 3 hdc, sc) into each ch-4 sp around, sl st in first sc to join.

Fasten off. Sew flower to hat. Using needle, weave in tail ends.

FLOWER (FOR HAT & SCARF)

SCARF

With I/9 (5.50mm) hook and two strands of MC held together, ch 150.

ROW 1: Hdc in 3rd ch from hook and in each ch across, turn—148 hdc total.

ROWS 2–6: Ch 2, hdc in each st across, turn.

Fasten off, leaving a 10" (25cm) tail. Use a yarn needle to weave in ends.

SCARF

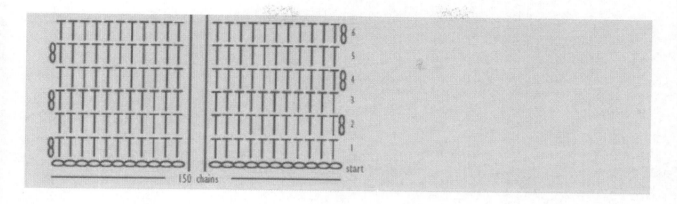

150 chains

FRINGE

Cut 48 10" (25cm) strands of MC. Hold four strands together, and fold them in half. Use hook to pull fold through edge of scarf at the end of each row. Pull fringe ends through the folded loop. Pull to tighten. Attach fringe to each row on both ends of Scarf. Trim fringe evenly.

FLOWER

Create a second flower, as for the Hat Flower, but keep working until the Flower measures 4" (10cm) in diameter.

Band

With F/5 (3.75mm) hook and CC, ch 11.

ROW 1: Sc in second ch from hook, turn.

ROWS 2–4: Ch 1, sc in each st across, turn.

Fasten off, leaving a 10" (25cm) tail. Using yarn needle, weave in ends. Sew the band onto the back of the flower.

FLOWER BAND

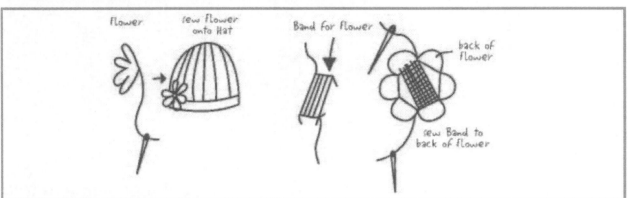

disco

glitter hat

This hat is made with double crochet and shell stitch. Typically, shell stitches are used for edging. Using this stitch and the yarn makes the hat an original piece. Who needs a disco ball when you have glittery yarn?

yarn

1 skein Patons Brilliant (acrylic/nylon/polyester blend, 166 yds ea) in color #3314 Lilac Luster

hooks and notions

size I/9 (5.5mm) hook

If necessary, change hook size to obtain gauge.

yarn needle

stitch marker

gauge

13 dc x 6½ rows = 4" (10cm)

finished size

23" (58cm) around x 8" (20cm) tall

notes

This pattern is worked in the round without joining. Place a marker in the last stitch of each round to mark the end of the round. Do not turn at the end of each round.

HAT

With MC, ch 4, sl st in first ch to form ring.

RND 1: Ch 3 (counts as first dc), work 12 dc into ring, place marker in last st to mark end of rnd. Do not join in first st—13 dc total.

RND 2: Work 2 dc in each st around, replace marker in last st throughout pattern —26 dc total.

RND 3: *Dc in next st, 2 dc in next st; rep from* around—39 dc total.

RND 4: *Dc in each of next 2 sts, 2 dc in next st; rep from* around—52 dc total.

RND 5: *Dc in each of next 3 sts, 2 dc in next st; rep from* around—65 dc total.

RND 6: *Sk 2 sts, 5 dc in next st, sk 2 sts, sc in next st; rep from* around, ending sk 1 st, sc in last st.

RND 7: *Sk first 2 dc of next 5-dc group, sc in next dc (center of 5-dc group), sk next 2 dc, 5 dc in next sc; rep from* around.

RNDS 8–13: Cont in a spiral, working sc in 3rd dc of each 5-dc group and 5 dc in each sc.

Sl st in next st. Fasten off, leaving a long tail for weaving in ends. Use a yarn needle to weave in ends.

HAT

RND 1 .... 13DC

2 .... 26DC

3 .... 39DC

4 .... 52DC

5 .... 65DC

6-13 5DC + 1SC ALL AROUND

snowball fight

mittens

This design is great for snowball fights. I suggest you make the thumb part first. When you are ready to attach the thumb, turn the thumb inside out before you single crochet in the first seven stitches. Follow the instructions and once the mitten body is done, you can finish attaching the thumb with woven seams for the remaining eleven stitches.

yarn

1 skein Dale of Norway Dale Baby Ull (100% wool, 192 yds ea) in color #9436 Kiwi (MC) 1 skein Dale of Norway Dale Baby Ull (100% wool, 192 yds ea) in color #20 Off White (CC)

hooks and notions

size F/5 (3.75mm) hook

If necessary, change hook size to obtain gauge.

stitch marker

yarn needle

gauge

21 sc x 19 rows = 4" (10cm)

finished size

7½" (19cm) long x 6½" (17cm) around wrist

Thumbs measure 2½" (6cm) long

notes

This pattern is worked in the round without joining. Place a marker in the last stitch of each round to mark the end of the round. Do not turn at the end of each round.

THUMBS (make 2)

With CC, ch 3, sl st in first ch to form ring.

RND 1: Ch 1, 5 sc into ring, place marker in last st to mark end of rnd. Do not join in first st—5 sc total.

RND 2: Work 2 sc in each sc around, replace marker in last st throughout pattern —10 sc total.

RND 3: *Sc in next st, 2 sc in next st; rep from* around— 15 sc total.

RND 4: Sc in each st around.

RNDS 5–8: Rep Rnd 4.

RND 9: *Sc in each of the next 4 sts, 2 sc in next st; rep from* around—18 sc total.

RNDS 10–18: Rep Rnd 4.

Sl st in next st. Fasten off, leaving a 10" (25cm) tail. Use a yarn needle to weave in ends.

THUMBS

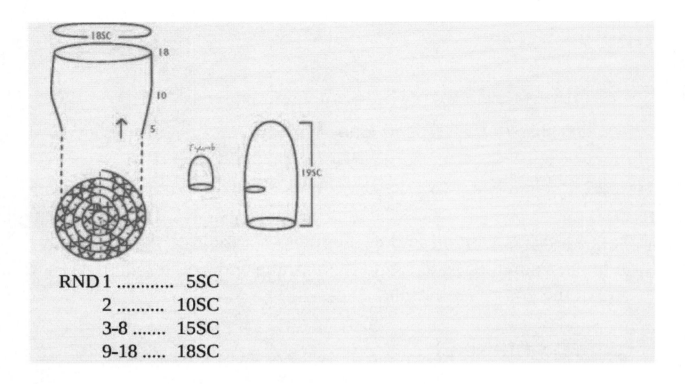

RND 1 .... 5SC
    2 .... 10SC
  3-8 .... 15SC
 9-18 ..... 18SC

BODY (make 2)

With MC, ch 4, sl st in first ch to form ring.

RND 1: Ch 1, 10 sc into ring, place marker in last st to mark end of rnd. Do not join in first st—10 sc total.

RND 2: Work 2 sc in each sc around, replace marker in last st throughout pattern —20 sc total.

RNDS 3–4: Sc in each st around.

RND 5: *Sc in next st, 2 sc in next st; rep from* around— 30 sc total.

RNDS 6–7: Rep Rnd 3.

RND 8: *Sc in each of next 2 sts, 2sc in next st; rep from* around—40 sc total.

RNDS 9–17: Rep Rnd 3.

RND 18: *2 sc in next st, sc in each of next 19 sts; rep from* once—42 sc total.

RNDS 19–36: Rep Rnd 3.

Join Thumb to Body

Turn Thumb inside out.

RND 37: With Thumb and Body held together and working through both thicknesses, sc in each of next 7 sts. Working in Body only, sc in each st around —42 sc total.

RND 38: Skip first 7 sc and ch 11 (rem Thumb sts). Working in Body only, sc in each st around—48 sc total.

RNDS 39–43: Rep Body Rnd 3—48 sc.

RND 44: Dec, sc in each of next 19 sts, dec, sc in each rem st around—46 sc total.

RNDS 45–46: Rep Rnd 3.

RND 47: Rep Rnd 44—44 sc total.

RNDS 48–56: Rep Rnd 3.

Sl st in next st. Fasten off, leaving a 10" (25cm) tail. Use a yarn needle to weave in ends. With MC and yarn needle, sew Thumb onto the ch 11 space at Rnd 38.

BODY

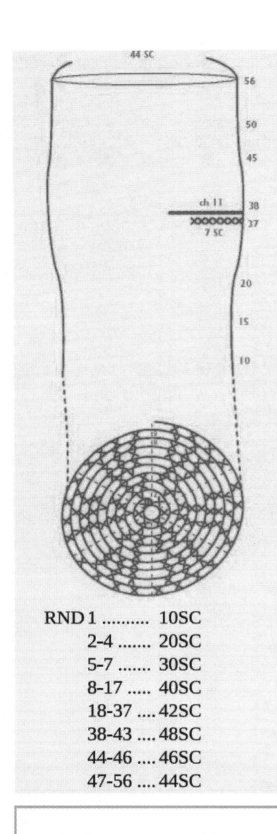

RND 1 .... 10SC
2-4 .... 20SC
5-7 .... 30SC
8-17 ..... 40SC
18-37 .... 42SC
38-43 .... 48SC
44-46 .... 46SC
47-56 .... 44SC

SPECIAL STITCH

Dec: insert hook in next st, yo and draw up loop, insert hook in following st, yo and draw up loop, yo and draw through all 3 loops on hook.

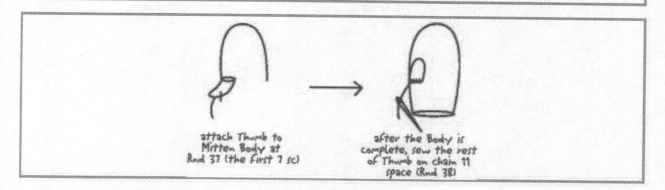

attach Thumb to
Mitten Body at
Rnd 37 (the first 7 sc)

after the Body is
complete, sew the rest
of Thumb on chain 11
space (Rnd 38)

romantic

mohair hat

This hat has a romantic spirit. The mohair yarn gives it a lovely feel, and the brim is made with a chain of loops that softens the hat. Place the flower over the area where you change to a different color to mask the color flaw.

yarn

1 skein Classic Elite La Gran (mohair/wool/nylon blend, 90 yds ea) in color #6542 Lavender Ice (MC) 1 skein Classic Elite La Gran (mohair/wool/nylon blend, 90 yds ea) in color #6554 French Lilac (CC)

hooks and notions

size I/9 (5.5mm) hook

If necessary, change hook size to obtain gauge.

stitch marker

yarn needle

gauge

13 dc x 5 rows = 4" (10cm)

finished size

21½" (55cm) around x 10" (25cm) tall, including brim

Flower measures 4" (10cm) in diameter

notes

This pattern is worked in the round without joining. Place a marker in the last stitch of each round to mark the end of the round. Do not turn at the end of each round.

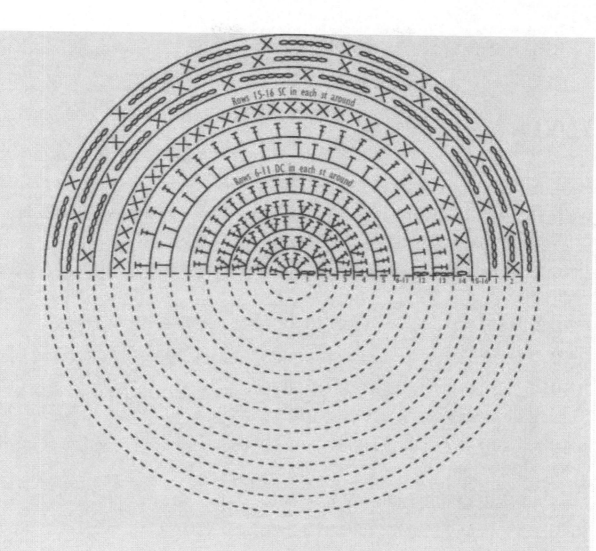

Rows 15-16 SC in each st around

Rows 6-11 DC in each st around

HAT

RND 1 .... 13DC

2 .... 26DC

3 .... 39DC

4-11 ..... 52DC

12 .... 52HDC

13 .... 52DC

14 .... 52SC

15-16 .... 52SC

BRIM

HAT

With MC, ch 4, sl st in first ch to form ring.

RND 1: Ch 3 (counts as first dc), work 12 dc into ring, place marker in last st to mark end of rnd. Do not join in first st—13 dc total.

RND 2: Work 2 dc in each st around, replace marker in last st throughut pattern —26 dc total.

RND 3: *Dc in next st, 2 dc in next st; rep from* around— 39 dc total.

RND 4: *Dc in each of next 2 sts, 2 dc in next st; rep from* around—52 dc total.

RNDS 5–11: Dc in each st around to last dc.

Sl st in next st. Fasten off, leaving a long tail.

RND 12: Joining CC, ch 2 (counts as hdc), hdc in each st around, sl st in 2nd ch of beg ch-2 to join.

Fasten off, leaving a long tail.

RND 13: Joining MC, ch 3 (counts as dc), dc in each st around, sl st in 3rd ch of beg ch-3 to join.

RNDS 14–16: Ch 1, sc in each st around, sl st in first sc to join.

Do not fasten off.

BRIM

RND 1: Ch 6, sk first 2 sts, sc in next st, *ch 6, sk next 2 sts, sc in next st; rep from* around, ending sc in second to last st. Do not join to beg of rnd.

RNDS 2–3: *Ch 6, sc into next ch-6 sp; rep from* around.

Fasten off, leaving a long tail. Use a yarn needle to weave in ends.

FLOWER

With CC, leave an approx 19" (48cm) tail at the beg, ch 4, sl st in first ch to form ring.

RND 1: Ch 5 (counts as dc and 2 chs), *dc into ring, ch 2; rep from* 4 times, sl st in 1st ch of beg ch-5 to join.

RND 2: Ch 1, work (sc, 2 hdc, dc, 2 hdc, sc) into each ch-2 sp around, sl st in first sc to join, turn—6 petals total.

RND 3: Working behind petals, (ch 3, sl st between petals) 6 times, sl st in 1st ch of beg ch-3 to join, turn.

RND 4: Ch 1, work (sc, 2 hdc, 3 dc, 2 hdc, sc) into each ch-3 sp around, sl st in first sc to join, turn.

RND 5: Working behind petals, (ch 4, sl st between petals) 6 times, sl st in 1st ch of beg ch-4 to join, turn.

RND 6: Ch 1, work (sc, 3 hdc, 4 dc, 3 hdc, sc) into each ch-4 sp around, sl st in first sc to join.

Fasten off, leaving a long tail for sewing.

Use a yarn needle to sew the flower to the hat. Weave in ends to finish.

FLOWER

matching mother-daughter

hats

This is a great pattern for a special mother-daughter outing. I prefer to use a multicolor, bulky yarn. And both hats can be made in three hours. A little tip: A mannequin head can be used to help put on the flower.

yarn

3 skeins Lion Brand Yarn Landscapes (wool/acrylic blend, 55 yds ea) in #271 Rose Garden *2 skeins for Mother Hat; 1 skein for Daughter Hat*

hooks and notions

size I/9 (5.5mm) hook

size G/6 (4.50mm) hook

If necessary, change hook size to obtain gauge.

stitch marker

yarn needle

gauge

12 dc x 4 rows = 4" (10cm) with larger hook

15 dc x 4½ rows = 4" (10cm) with smaller hook

finished size

Mother Hat

22" (56cm) around x 9½" (24cm) tall

Flower measures 4" (10cm) in diameter

Daughter Hat

18" (46cm) around x 6½" (17cm) tall

Flower measures 3½" (9cm) in diameter

notes

This pattern is worked in the round without joining. Place a marker in the last stitch of each round to mark the end of the round. Do not turn at the end of each round.

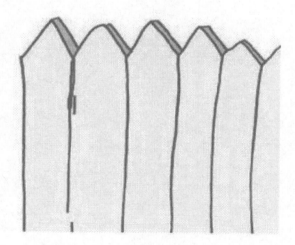

MOTHER HAT

With larger hook, ch 4, form ring by joining with sl st to the 4th ch from hook.

RND 1: Ch 3 (counts as first dc), work 12 dc into ring, place marker in last st to mark end of rnd. Do not join in first st—13 dc total.

RND 2: Work 2 dc in each st around, replace marker in last st throughout pattern —26 dc total.

RND 3: *Dc in next st, 2 dc in next st; rep from* around—39 dc total.

RND 4: *Dc in each of next 2 sts, 2 dc in next st; rep from* around—52 dc total.

RNDS 5–9: Dc in each st around.

RND 10: Dc in each st around to last st, sl st in last st.

RND 11: Ch 3, dc in each st around, sl st in 3rd ch of beg ch-3.

RNDS 12–14: Ch 1, sc in each st around, sl st in first sc to join.

Fasten off, leaving a long tail. Use a yarn needle to weave in ends.

MOTHER HAT

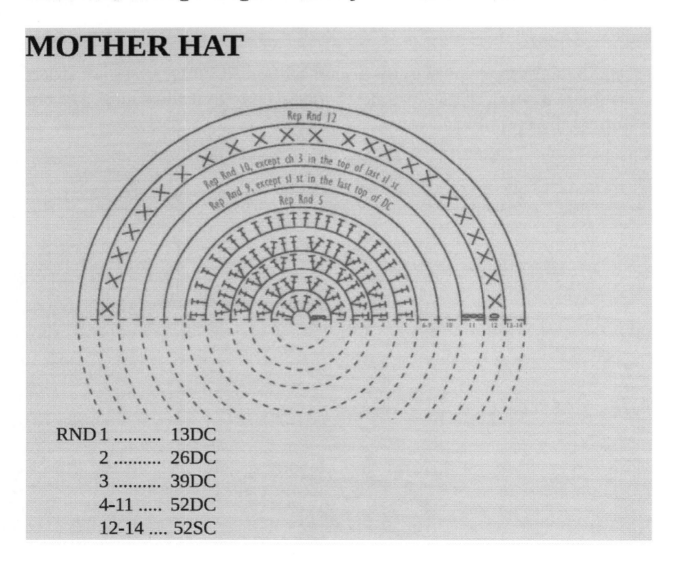

```
RND 1 .......... 13DC
     2 .......... 26DC
     3 .......... 39DC
  4-11 ..... 52DC
 12-14 .... 52SC
```

FLOWER (for Mother Hat)

Leaving an approx 19" (48cm) tail, with larger hook ch 4, sl st in first ch to form ring.

RND 1: Ch 5 (counts as dc, ch 2), work (dc, ch 2) into ring 5 times, sl st in 3rd ch of beg ch-5 to join.

RND 2: Ch 1, work (sc, 2 hdc, dc, 2 hdc, sc) into each ch-2 space around, sl st in first sc to join, turn.

RND 3: Working behind petals, (ch 3, sl st) 5 times, ch 3, sl st in first ch of beg ch-3, turn.

RND 4: Ch 1, work (sc, 2 hdc, 3 dc, 2 hdc, sc) into each ch-3 sp around, sl st in first sc to join.

Fasten off, leaving a long tail for sewing.

MOTHER HAT FLOWER

DAUGHTER HAT

With smaller hook, ch 4, sl st in first ch to form ring.

RND 1: Ch 3 (counts as first dc), work 11 dc into ring, place marker in last st to mark end of rnd. Do not join in first st—12 dc total.

RND 2: Work 2 dc in each st around, replace marker in last st throughout pattern —24 dc total.

RND 3: *Dc in next st, 2 dc in next st; rep from* around—36 dc total.

RND 4: *Dc in each of next 2 sts, 2 dc in next st; rep from* around—48 dc total.

RNDS 5–7: Dc in each st around.

RND 8: Dc in each st to last st, sl st in last st.

RND 9: Ch 1, sc in each st around, sl st in first sc to join.

RNDS 10–11: Ch 1, sc in each st around, sl st in first sc to join.

Fasten off, leaving a long tail. Use a yarn needle to weave in ends.

DAUGHTER HAT

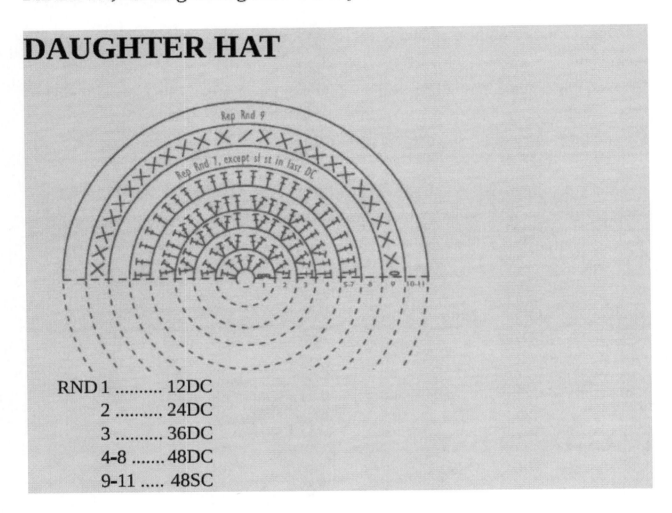

RND 1 .... 12DC
2 .... 24DC
3 .... 36DC
4-8 .... 48DC
9-11 ..... 48SC

FLOWER (for Daughter Hat)

Leaving an approx 15" (38cm) tail end, with smaller hook ch 4, sl st in first ch to form ring.

RND 1: Ch 5 (counts as dc, ch 2), work (dc, ch 2) into ring 5 times, sl st in 3rd ch of beg ch-5 to join.

RND 2: Ch 1, work (sc, 2 hdc, dc, 2 hdc, sc) into each ch-2 space around, sl st in first sc to join.

Fasten off, leaving a long tail for sewing.

DAUGHTER HAT FLOWER

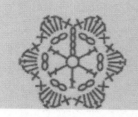

Assembly

For both Mother and Daughter Hats, use the long tail from the Flower and a yarn needle to sew the Flower to the hat. Weave in ends.

No more grandma's granny square! Grab some inspiration from the 1970s and make it contemporary. You can even improvise with the square motifs and mass-produce them to make a pillowcase or blanket. Once you learn the pattern, you can use different colors and yarn to spice it up.

yarn

1 skein Lion Brand Wool-Ease (acrylic/wool blend, 197 yds ea) in #98 Natural Heather (MC) 1 skein each of Lion Brand Wool-Ease (acrylic/wool blend, 197 yds ea) in #153 Black (CC1), #151 Grey Heather (CC2), #152 Oxford Grey (CC3)

hooks and notions

size G/6 (4.50mm) hook

If necessary, change hook size to obtain gauge.

yarn needle

gauge

15 dc x 6 rows = 4" (10cm)

finished size

43" (109cm) long x 10½" (27cm) wide, excluding fringe

Each square measures 5" (13cm)

SQUARES (make 16 A and 16 B)

Follow the pattern as given to make Square A. The colors used for Square B are indicated in brackets.

With MC [CC2], ch 4, sl st in first ch to form ring.

RND 1: Ch 3, (counts as dc), 2 dc into ring, ch 4, work (3 dc, ch 4) into ring 3 times—12 dc total.

RND 2: Joining CC1 [CC3], ch 5 (counts as dc, ch 2), skip

scarf hoodie

first 3 dc, *work (3 dc, ch 4, 3 dc) all into ch-4 sp, ch 2, skip next 3 dc; rep from* 2 times, work (3 dc, ch 4, 2 dc) all into last ch-4 sp, sl st in 3rd ch of beg ch-3 to join.

RND 3: Joining CC2 [CC1], ch 3 (counts as dc), 2 dc in first ch-2 sp, ch 2, skip next 3 dc, *work (3 dc, ch 4, 3 dc) all into ch-4 sp, ch 2, skip next 3 dc, 3 dc into next ch-2 sp, ch 2, skip next 3 dc; rep from* 2 times, work (3 dc, ch 4, 3 dc) all into last ch-4 sp, ch 2, sl st in 3rd ch of beg ch-3.

RND 4: Joining CC3 [MC], ch 5 (counts as dc, ch 2), skip first 2 dc, *3 dc in next ch-2 sp, ch 2, skip next 3 dc, work (3 dc, ch 4, 3 dc) all into ch-4 sp, [ch 2, skip next 3 dc, 3 dc into next ch-2 sp] twice, ch 2, skip next 3 dc; rep from* 2 times, work (3 dc, ch 4, 3 dc) all into last ch-4 sp, ch 2, 2 dc in last ch-2 sp, sl st in 3rd ch of beg ch-3.

Fasten off, leaving a long tail for sewing. Use a yarn needle to weave in ends.

SQUARE

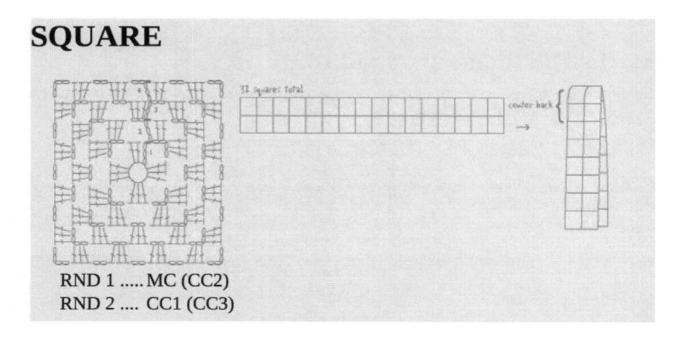

RND 1 ..... MC (CC2)
RND 2 .... CC1 (CC3)

RND 3 .... CC2 (CC1)
RND 4 ..... CC3 (MC)

Assembly

With right sides facing, sew one side of two squares together, alternating between Square A and Square B. Continue to add squares until you have one long strip of 16 squares. Make a second strip of 16 squares in the same manner. Join strips together along one long edge. Fold the scarf in half widthwise to find the center. Sew the back edge of two squares on one side of the fold to two squares on the other side of the fold to create the hood. Add fringe to both ends.

striped hat, scarf and

wristband set

My good friend loves stripes. If it has a stripe in it, she wants to wear it. This matching set is sporty with a feminine flair. One important detail here is the edging on the flower—the different color makes the flower really stand out. Choose your own favorite colors for these projects, if you like. The wristbands in this set are the pièce de résistance. Wonder Woman did it best with her golden, bullet-proof wristbands, but this pattern gives you a chance to create some superpowers of your own. Jazz up the wristbands with different buttons and snaps or even some velcro. The 1970s would be so proud.

yarn

1 skein Cascade Yarns Cascade 220 (100% Peruvian highland wool, 220 yds ea) in color #8234 Green (MC)

1 skein each of Cascade Yarns Cascade 200 (100% Peruvian highland wool, 220 yds ea) in color #8010 Ivory (CC1), color #8412 Yellow (CC2), and color #2415 Mustard (CC3)

If making all three pieces in set, purchase two skeins of each color.

hooks and notions

size G/6 (4.50mm) hook

If necessary, change hook size to obtain gauge.

stitch marker

yarn needle

sewing needle

gauge

Hat

15 dc x 6½ rows = 4" (10cm)

Scarf

15 dc x 7 rows = 4" (10cm)

Wristband

17 dc x 7 rows = 4" (10cm)

finished sizes

Hat

22" (56cm) around x 7" (18cm) tall

Scarf

40" (102cm) long x 4" (10cm) wide

Wristband

7½" (19cm) around x 4½" (12cm) wide

notes

Please refer to the individual patterns for instructions on which rounds should be joined.

HAT

With MC, ch 4, sl st in first ch to form ring.

RND 1: Ch 3 (counts as first dc), work 12 dc into ring, place marker in last st to mark end of rnd. Do not join in first st—13 dc total.

RND 2: Work 2 dc in each st around, replace marker in last st throughout pattern —26 dc total.

RND 3: *Dc in next st, 2 dc in next st; rep from* around—39 dc total.

RND 4: *Dc in each of next 2 sts, 2 dc in next st; rep from* around—52 dc total.

RND 5: *Dc in each of next 3 sts, 2 dc in next st; rep from* around—65 dc total.

RNDS 6–11: Dc in each st around.

RND 12: Dc in each st around to last st, sl st in last st.

RND 13: Joining CC1, ch 2 (counts as hdc), hdc in each st around, sl st in 2nd ch of beg ch-2 to join.

RND 14: Joining CC2, ch 2 (counts as hdc), hdc in each st around, sl st in 2nd ch of beg ch-2 to join.

RND 15: Joining CC3, ch 2 (counts as hdc), hdc in each st around, sl st in 2nd ch of beg ch-2 to join.

RND 16: Joining MC, ch 3 (counts as dc), dc in each st around, sl st in 3rd ch of beg ch-3 to join.

RND 17: Ch 1, sc in each st around, sl st in first sc to join.

RNDS 18–19: Rep Rnd 17.

Fasten off, leaving a long tail. Use a yarn needle to weave in ends.

HAT

RND 1 .... 13DC (MC)
   2 .... 26DC
   3 .... 39DC
   4 .... 52DC
   5-12 ..... 65DC
   13 .... 65HDC (CC1)
   14 .... 65HDC (CC2)
   15 .... 65HDC (CC3)
   16 .... 65DC (CC1)
   17-19 .... 65SC

COLOR KEY

MC GREEN
CC1 IVORY
CC2 YELLOW
CC3 MUSTARD

FLOWER (for Hat)

Leaving an approx 19" (48cm) tail of CC2, ch 4, sl st in first ch to form ring.

RND 1: Ch 5 (counts as dc, ch 2), work (dc, ch 2) into ring 5 times, sl st in 3rd ch of beg ch-5 to join—6 ch-2 spaces total.

RND 2: Ch 1, work (sc, 2 hdc, dc, 2 hdc, sc) into each ch-2 sp around, sl st in first sc to join—6 petals total.

RND 3: Attach CC3, ch 1, sc in same st as join, sc in each of next 2 sts, 2 sc in next st (center of petal), sc in each of next 3 sts, *sc in each of next 3 sts, 2 sc in next st, sc in each of next 3 sts; rep from* around, sl st in first sc to join.

Fasten off, leaving long tail for sewing.

HAT FLOWER

FINISHING

Use the long tail and a yarn needle to sew the flower to the hat. Weave in ends.

WRISTBAND

With MC, ch 29.

ROW 1: Hdc in 3rd ch from hook and in each ch across, turn—27 hdc total.

ROW 2: Joining CC1, ch 3, dc in first st and in each st across, do not work in turning ch, turn.

ROW 3: Joining CC2, ch 3, dc in first st and in each st across, do not work in turning ch, turn.

ROW 4: Joining CC3, ch 2, hdc in first st and in each st across, do not work in turning ch, turn.

ROW 5: Joining MC, ch 2, hdc in first st and in each of next 3 sts, *2 hdc in next st, hdc in each of next 5 sts; rep from* across, ending hdc in each of last 4 sts, do not work in turning ch, turn—31 hdc total.

ROWS 6–8: Rep Rows 2–4.

Do not fasten off.

WRISTBAND

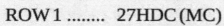

ROW 1 .... 27HDC (MC)
    2 .... 27DC (CC1)
    3 .... 27DC (CC2)
    4 .... 27HDC (CC3)
    5 .... 31HDC (MC)
    6 .... 31DC (CC1)
    7 .... 31DC (CC2)
    8 .... 31HDC (CC3)

COLOR KEY

MC GREEN
CC1 IVORY
CC2 YELLOW
CC3 MUSTARD

BUTTON BAND

Turn wristband one-quarter-turn clockwise so that row ends are on top. Ch 3, dc in end of first row, work 13 dc evenly across. Sew on three evenly-spaced buttons using MC and sewing needle.

SCARF

With MC, ch 150.

ROW 1: Dc in 4th ch from hook and in each ch across, turn—147 dc total.

ROWS 2–4: Ch 3, dc in each st across, turn.

ROW 5: Joining CC1, ch 2, hdc in each st across, turn.

ROW 6: Joining CC2, ch 2, hdc in each st across, turn.

ROW 7: Joining CC3, ch 2, hdc in each st across, turn.

Fasten off, leaving a long tail. Use a yarn needle to weave in ends.
Add fringe to both ends of the scarf.

SCARF

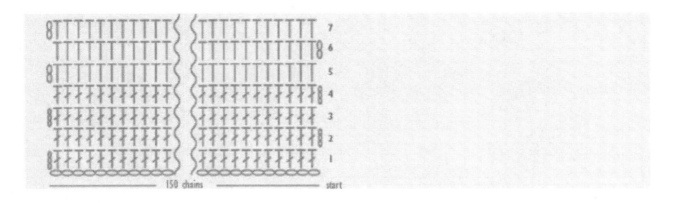

150 chains — start

FLOWER (for Scarf)

With CC2, ch 4, sl st in first ch to form ring.

RND 1: Ch 5 (counts as dc, ch 2), work (dc, ch 2) into ring 5 times, sl st in 3rd ch of beg ch-5 to join—6 dc-2 spaces total.

RND 2: Ch 1, work (sc, hdc, 3 dc, hdc, sc) into each ch-2 sp around, sl st in first sc to join—6 petals total.

RND 3: Joining CC3, ch 1, sc in same st as join, sc in each of next 2 sts, 2 sc in next st (center of petal), sc in each of next 3 sts, *sc in each of next 3 sts, 2 sc in next st, sc in each of next 3 sts; rep from* around, sl st in first sc to join.

RND 4: Joining CC2, turn, work (ch 3, sl st in sp between petals) 5 times, ending ch 3, sl st in 1st ch of beg ch-3 to join.

RND 5: Turn, ch 1, work (sc, hdc, 5 dc, hdc, sc) into each ch-3 sp around, sl st in first sc to join.

RND 6: Joining CC3, ch 1, sc in same st as join, sc in each of next 2 sts, 2 sc in each of next 3 sts, sc in each of next 3 sts, *sc in each of next 3 sts, 2 sc in each of next 3 sts, sc in each of next 3 sts; rep from* around, sl st in first sc to join.

RND 7: Joining CC2, turn, work (ch 4, sl st in sp between petals) 5 times, ending ch 4, sl st in 1st ch of beg ch-4 to join.

RND 8: Turn, ch 1, work (sc, 2 hdc, 6 dc, 2 hdc, sc) into each ch-4 sp around, sl st in first sc to join.
Fasten off.

RND 9: Joining CC3, ch 1, sc in same st as join, sc in each of next 3 sts, 2 sc in each of next 4 sts, sc in each of next 4 sts, *sc in each of next 4 sts, 2 sc in each of next 4 sts, sc in each of next 4 sts; rep from* around, sl st in first sc to join.

Fasten off, leaving a long tail for sewing. Use a yarn needle to weave in ends.

SCARF FLOWER

BAND (for back of Flower)

Leaving an approx 10" (25cm) tail of CC2, ch 11.

ROW 1: Sc in 2nd ch from hook and in each ch across, turn—10 sc total.

ROWS 2–4: Ch 1, sc in each st across, turn.

Fasten off, leaving a long tail for sewing. Use a yarn needle to weave in ends.

FLOWER BAND

Finishing

Slide the flower onto the scarf, then wrap the scarf around your neck and slide the free end through the loop in the back of the flower to secure the scarf.

Fringe

Cut 56 10" (25cm) strands of MC. Hold four strands together and fold them in half. Use a hook to pull the fold through the edge of the scarf at the end of each row. Pull fringe ends through the folded loop. Pull to tighten. Attach fringe to each row on both ends of scarf. Trim fringe evenly.

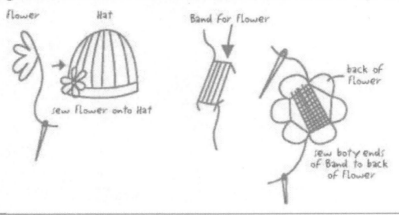

geometric

earrings

This project can be made out of any extra scrap yarn. If you are a fast crocheter, you can finish a pair of earrings within fifteen minutes. Make your own personalized earrings by using different colors of crystals or lightweight beads.

Triangle Earrings

yarn

1 spool Lion Brand Lamé (metalized polyester/rayon blend, 75 yds ea) in #153 Black

hooks and notions

size C/2 (2.75mm) hook

If necessary, change hook size to obtain gauge.

4 silver jump rings

2 silver earring hooks

gauge

25 chs x 37 rows = 4" (10cm)

finished size

1¾" (5cm)

Square Earrings

yarn

1 spool Lion Brand Lamé (metalized polyester/rayon blend, 75 yds ea) in color #150 Silver

hooks and notions

size C/2 (2.75mm) hook

If necessary, change hook size to obtain gauge.

4 silver jump rings

2 silver earring hooks

2 Swarovski Crystal beads

finished size

1½" (4cm)

Flower Earrings

yarn

1 spool Lion Brand Lamé (metalized polyester/rayon blend, 75 yds ea) in color #303 Multi

hooks and notions

size C/2 (2.75mm) hook

If necessary, change hook size to obtain gauge.

4 silver jump rings

2 silver earring hooks

2 Swarovski Crystal beads

fabric glue

gauge

25 chs x 37 rows= 4" (10cm)

finished size

2" (5cm)

TRIANGLE EARRINGS (make 2) Ch 5, sl st in first ch to form ring.

RND 1: Ch 3 (counts as dc), 2 dc into ring, (ch 5, 3 dc) into ring twice, ch 2, dc into 3rd ch of beg ch-3 to join.

RND 2: Ch 3 (counts as dc), 2 dc in sp made by joining dc, *ch 3, 3 dc in next ch-5 sp, ch 5, 3 dc in same ch-5 sp; rep from* once, ch 3, 3 dc in next ch-2 sp, ch 5, sl st in 3rd ch of beg ch-3 to join.

Fasten off and weave in ends.

TRIANGLE EARRINGS

FINISHING

Connect two silver jump rings together. Attach one end of the jump rings to any ch-5 sp.

Attach the other end of the jump rings to the earring hook.

SQUARE EARRINGS (make 2)

Ch 6, sl st in first ch to form ring.

RND 1: Ch 3 (counts as dc), 3 dc into ring, work (ch 3, 4 dc) into ring 3 times, ch 3, sl st in 3rd ch of beg ch-3 to join.

RND 2: Ch 2 (counts as dc), work dc dec over next 3 sts, *work (ch 3, 2-dc cluster) twice into next ch-3 sp, ch 3, dc dec over next 4 sts; rep from* 2 times, work (ch 3, 2-dc cluster) twice into last ch-3 sp, ch 3, sl st in first cluster to join.

Fasten off and weave in ends.

SQUARE EARRINGS

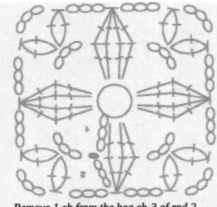

Remove 1 ch from the beg ch-3 of rnd 2.
Beg dc clusters start with a ch-2.

FINISHING

Connect two silver jump rings together.

Attach one end of jump rings to any corner ch-3 sp. Attach the other end of the jump rings to the earring hook. Attach a Swarovski crystal to center of each motif.

SPECIAL STITCHES

2-dc Cluster: Yo, insert hook in st, yo, pull through st, yo, pull through 2 lps on hook, yo, insert hook in same st, yo, pull through st, yo, pull through 2 lps on hook, yo, pull through all lps on hook.

dc dec: yo, insert hook in first st, yo, pull through st, yo, pull through 2 lps on hook, (yo, insert hook in next st, yo, pull through st, yo, pull through 2 lps on hook) as many times as directed, yo, pull through all lps on hook.

FLOWER EARRINGS (make 2)

Ch 6, sl st in first ch to form ring.

RND 1: Ch 1, 8 sc into ring, sl st in first sc to join.

RND 2: Ch 2 (counts as dc), dc in same st as join, *ch 4, 2-dc cluster in next st; rep from* 6 times, ch 2, hdc in first dc to join.

RND 3: Ch 1, sc in sp made by joining hdc, ch 5, *work (sc, ch 5 twice) into next ch-4 sp; rep from* around 6 times, sc into next ch-2 sp, ch 5, sl st in first sc to join.

Fasten off and weave in ends.

FLOWER EARRINGS

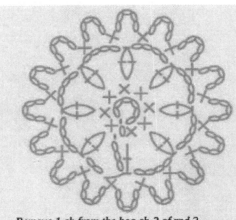

Remove 1 ch from the beg ch-3 of rnd 2.
Beg dc clusters start with a ch-2.

FINISHING

Connect two silver jump rings together. Attach one end of the jump rings to any sc between ch-5 spaces. Attach the other end of the jump rings to the earring hook. Glue a Swarovski crystal to the center of each motif.

Made in United States
Orlando, FL
23 August 2024

50696116R00115